REDEFINING ORGANISATIONAL EXCELLENCE

STRAIGHT TALK ON PERFORMANCE AND PROFIT MAXIMISATION STRATEGIES!

DR. AMIT DAS

To

All my bosses and mentors who made a difference in my professional career.

"The excellence of an organisation are ultimately the consequence of the contributions made by each individual."

- Dr. Amit Das, Motivational Speaker, Leadership Coach , Counsellor, and Mentor.

Contents

Foreword

Dear Readers,

Thank you for taking your precious time to learn more about **"Redefining Organisational Excellence"**. This book aims to give you a plan to recognise, prevent, and resolve workplace challenges, whether your business is already on its way to the top of the healthy workplace culture pyramid or you're beginning from scratch. And whether you're a leader, an aspiring leader, or an employee looking to avoid unnecessary drama, the advice in this book will help you contribute to the answer we're all looking for.

This multifold issue, according to the author, necessitates the development of an organisational excellence programme that fits and flourishes in these multicultural cultures. In response, he examines corporate practises in business excellence frameworks that have been widely employed to promote organisational performance on a global scale. Effective leadership practises are addressed in the book as a component that is no longer an option, but rather a need for organisations to succeed in more globalised markets.

Countless business professionals strive to be successful leaders. The actual aim for industrious, growth-oriented top performers who are never content with the status quo and rigorous thinkers who are never satisfied with the status quo is the lifetime pursuit of perfection. Dr. Amit Das has interviewed hundreds of the most prolific performers to learn the best strategies for pursuing and maintaining organisational greatness. He discovered a pattern of unusual actions that distinguished these exceptional people. You'll learn how to: commit to yourself and the process-and develop purpose, focus, and discipline; develop resilience to face new challenges and find inspiration for the long haul; seek guidance-and lead others to new heights; meet the moment-and make the most of every opportunity to excel; and build a trusted group of advisors-and become a lifelong learner by following his examples. With the pursuit of organisational excellence, you can put your attitudes into action and convert your actions into habits. You refer to this human yearning for greater and better things as the pursuit of human perfection. You all have the necessary tools to achieve greatness. They are, however, mainly inactive. You must make concerted efforts to reach your full potential.

This book, **"Redefining Organisational Excellence,"** is a new research and opportunity reference that looks at the link between corporate culture and commercial performance. This book is appropriate for business professionals, managers, researchers, and academicians, and it highlights subjects such as cultural excellence and individual productivity. When there is an organisational culture that aligns and motivates people; an effective strategy that delivers value in response to client priorities; processes and systems that produce efficient, high-quality work; an organisational structure that empowers people and facilitates workflow; and a strategy that recruits, develops, and retains the right people, the best results are produced. The correct balance between the total and the parts is found in a great organisation.

As a result, in order to be exceptional for a long time, an organisation must master the art of change management. This book is meant to give the necessary tools for attaining a deeper understanding of the key drivers of organisational excellence. In this book, **"Redefining Organisational**

Excellence," the author explores how to: excite and engage people; address problems that have a direct impact on your bottom line; distinguish between management and leadership; and assist employees in overcoming their toughest hurdles. The author also looks at whether great leaders are born or made, how lean ideas are used differently in various organisations, and why clever individuals fail so often after being promoted to management positions.

You will learn how to uncover your current cultural system, identify your target, brilliant culture, design solutions with participation from all organisational levels, develop action plans to instil new mindsets, behaviours, and structures, and make listening, trust, and truth-telling an essential part of your organisation by reading this book. The author provides businesses with a step-by-step strategy for analysing, creating, and implementing iterative cultural transformation, with each success building on prior achievements. As a result, the organisation continues to adapt in ways that reduce stress, encourage learning, and promote organisational wellness.

The book, **"Redefining Organisational Excellence,"** delves into how and where these efforts must be made in order for this to happen. This book is the result of the author's own endeavour to improve organisational performance. The most current concepts, as well as new observations and opinions, have been chosen and assembled. It will be extremely beneficial to the readers in their pursuit of perfection. The level of competition is rising. Internal dysfunctions hinder the ability to address important issues. There are no clearly defined strategies. Organisational procedures and structures aren't set up to supply the strategies that are required. Employees aren't aligned, motivated, or capable of delivering at a high level, and corporate cultures don't encourage competitive differentiation practises. The first and most important step to increasing morale is to focus on supporting and resourcing your employee. Remember, if you make the effort to create a great corporate culture, your organisation will prosper. A healthy culture is a typical feature of strong organisations. Your corporate culture is simply the way you operate together, the sum of your team's values and practises. The issue is that, whether you're paying attention or not. So, how can you nurture the culture you desire?

The book covers the numerous characteristics of organisational leadership and the implications they have on important outcomes such as employee behaviours, work satisfaction, team creativity and innovation, and organisational success, based on multiple rigorous research studies in Western and Eastern cultures. The book presents a measurement instrument that may be used for organisational culture evaluation, selection, and training, as well as developing strategies to exploit organisational leadership's behavioural aspects at the personal, team, and organisational levels.

Leadership must optimise alignment, competence, and engagement within their organisations more than ever before. Human resource planning and strategic talent management are used to convey and examine many aspects of global talent management to readers. Organisational executives and HR professionals who deal with talent management, today's most important business problem, must read this. This book offers a wealth of inspiring principles, methods, and models for formulating and putting into practise talent excellence strategies. This book's sections include cutting-edge methods, step-by-step useful management approaches, and informative resources that will enable you to find and nurture emerging talent; motivate; mentor; and prepare your future leaders.

Dr. Amit Das provides a step-by-step approach in this book, **"Redefining Organisational Excellence,"** on how to create an excellent culture at your organisation. The author demonstrates how to uncover your hidden culture, set up feedback loops, transform ideals into actions, and open up communication across layers. To keep your culture thriving for the long term, the author emphasises the significance of being clear from the top, building trust, and providing support structures. As Dr. Amit Das demonstrates in his book, by building your culture, you can increase communication, raise morale, encourage trust, and keep negativity at bay within your team. His insights and interviews from business sectors are used to demonstrate the obstacles to high performance and leadership.

The author of this book wants to provide you with a step-by-step guide to assist you in creating an excellent culture at your organisation. The author will discuss how to get your team on a mission together. He'll teach you how to communicate clearly from the top, create trust, and set up some support structures to keep your culture flourishing. Finally, the author will provide you with some hands-on ways to nourish your culture over time. So, if you're ready to make a change or transform your organisation.

Once again, thank you for taking the time to learn more about organisational excellence. Thank you for taking the time to read this book.

So, happy reading and learning to all my readers.

Carpe diem.

Dr. Amit Das

Leadership Coach , Counsellor, and Mentor.

Preface

"Excellence is not about being the greatest in the world; it is about being the best you can be and always pushing the boundaries."

Excellence is the result of continually achieving your best in all that you do. Excellence is the regular performance of ordinary things extremely well. To create awareness, create excellence, and follow through with excellence in execution goes above and beyond anything else on the market in terms of equipping leaders with the tools they need to become exceptional in execution. This book, a practical guide, will assist you in precisely assessing your organisation's present situation and developing a plan that will optimise its future success. I will expand on the power of understanding people by offering fresh applications, practical real-world techniques, and strong organisational evaluation tools, among other things.

As I sat down at my computer today to write a book about organisational excellence, transforming mediocrity into greatness and bringing out the best in people, I realised how much mediocrity envelops this nation, the ostensibly last frontier. Some of you are like fireflies in this darkness, with the will and capacity to shine small lights of greatness in your little corners. Whether it's boiling a cup of coffee, baking a loaf of bread, constructing a website, or developing a organisation development plan, how you do it reveals who you are to others around you. There is a significant difference between pushing the limits and doing what is adequate. So, wherever you are, the first step in building an atmosphere for greatness is to light up others by being an inspiration to them. This is called "lead by example."

This book attempts to provide insights into the many pathways, courses, and drives that world-class enterprises have constructed in order to achieve the pinnacles of greatness. It also includes an empirical analysis of leadership, a simple and practical conceptual model of what leadership is, and an actionable guide for developing competitive spirit, achieving sustained performance, achieving durable influencing capacity, assisting others in bringing change, and assisting in the actualisation of human potential in all roles and levels. It contains the ideas, views, experiences, beliefs, viewpoints, and forward-thinking thoughts of some of the best management and business minds in the world.

Recent business trends have caused organisations to undertake transformations at a faster rate than ever before, and as a result, the importance of human resources has grown. Though there has been extensive research in the field, with the changing paradigm, an attempt has been made through this book to determine the current state of organisations and examine the impact of an emerging aspect of the transformative cultural context on achieving organisational excellence in both the Indian and global contexts.

The purpose of this book is to comprehend the mechanisms that drive excellence as an organisational culture and how it should now be regarded in light of the coronavirus epidemic. To begin with, "good" enterprises must be recognised for what they are. Good businesses are usually well-run, efficient organisations with above-average financials that increase stakeholder value. So, what distinguishes an exceptional organisation from a good one? Superlative performance in all business operations is a vital objective for an amazing organisation. It promotes a culture of "going the extra mile" as a habit, making it second nature to all of its employees. It promotes the aphorism "do it right the first time, every time" as a basic organisational attitude.

Leadership alignment, leadership philosophy, corporate culture, employee experience, and customer experience are among the important aspects of organisational success discussed in the book. Each thorough chapter explains a fundamental component of peak performance culture, including a clear explanation, examples, expert insights, and practical considerations applicable to a variety of real-world scenarios. Employees appear to be more desirous of meaningful, purpose-driven employment than at any other moment in history. Big companies and social entrepreneurship have grown in popularity over the past decade. It's all over the news. Non-profits are no longer the only ones whose activities should result in some social good.

Employees want more from their employers than vague promises about community involvement and social responsibility. They seek businesses with a social mission, businesses that combine social benefit with commercial ambitions. Employees now have a clear mandate. Organisational excellence, according to the book, is a well-defined destination.

Organisations may structure their operations in such a way that they achieve and sustain excellence. With this system, any employee can detect any problem as soon as it arises and rectify it as quickly as possible so that activities may continue uninterrupted. The book lays out a step-by-step process for creating an ideal organisation, making organisational excellence simple to accomplish.

Whether your organisation is struggling with performance issues or is currently successful but aspires to even greater heights, a peak performance culture can help. Leaders now realise that they must be able to design strategy as well as execute it. However, practically all books, blogs, presentations, articles, and other materials focus on "why" execution is vital rather than "how" to execute well.

Today's top workers also have radically changed expectations for themselves and how they approach their jobs. Learn how to create and put into action a world-class talent plan that supports company goals and how to identify success measures. Talent is a precious and occasionally rare commodity, so talent management is becoming more and more crucial. While mid-level managers are still expected to recruit, engage, keep, and develop talent, most organisations focus most of their development resources on the C-suite. However, managing daily responsibilities while maintaining team performance and navigating obstacles leaves little time for management planning. In the framework of talent excellence, I take into account that talent is defined from the perspective of the organisation's core values in connection to the mission-critical employees whose value-add directly aids the organisation in realising its fundamental values.

Excellence in execution seeks to pick up where the majority of others drop off. It focuses on transforming leaders' present mindsets and attitudes. It is divided into two parts and takes the reader on a journey of implementation. Two-thirds of strategy of executions still fail, necessitating a new method. Strategy Cadence, execution juxtaposition, and deciphering the execution problem are some of the new words offered. It focuses on transforming leaders' present mindsets and attitudes. Create awareness, create excellence, and follow through with excellence in execution. This goes above and beyond anything else on the market in terms of equipping leaders with the tools they need to become exceptional in execution. Prepare for limited performance and poor outcomes if you're locked in an old leadership paradigm. With the pace of change increasing by the day, it's more critical than ever to cultivate a positive and enabling culture.

"The achievements of an organisation are the results of the combined effort of each individual."

This book presents a research-based, actionable methodology and metric for measuring organisational excellence to assist managers in creating productive and results-oriented workplaces. It explains why the top organisations in the world, such as Starbucks, Southwest Airlines, Amazon, Google, and Apple, thrive in leadership. Organisational excellence is a thought-provoking and emotionally rewarding philosophy of organisational transformation that has relevance and application in the workplace.

This book is also about you—there are so many different aspects of your existence in the complicated world you live in: internal, external, and personal life; family life, job life, professional life, and social life. Each aspect of life has its own set of challenges and worries. You are not a single homogeneous bunch, either. You belong to a variety of organisations and have a variety of identities, including economic, political, social, religious, cultural, national, racial, and so on. Despite all of your differences and similarities, there are many things that you all share in common. Above all, you are all human beings. Human senses and sensibilities are identical within you. Everyone has the ability to feel, think, experience, and reflect. You all want to live in a more comfortable and delightful environment, and you all want to improve, progress, and improve your life. The final aim remains the same, whether you're an aspiring leader or an entrepreneur: to realise your full potential, you all want to improve, progress, and improve your lives.

"A mind full of ideas only can think of achieving excellence; in any field one aspires to do remarkable thing in the world; dreams only generate ideas to such an active mind of a person; to realise all dreams one day or other in the world of chances!"

I will offer the most effective tactics and step-by-step instructions for you to construct your own particular road to excellence in this book. You'll learn how to concentrate on achieving greatness while living and enjoying life to the fullest. You'll develop a more optimistic attitude, more concentrated dedication, better ways to deal with distractions and demands, and tactics for conquering challenges. You'll also find better methods to collaborate with colleagues, respond more effectively to coaching and mentoring, and become more positive and self-directed in your thoughts and actions, resulting in more personal and professional pleasure. Although particular criteria may change over time, few goals in education are considered more essential than achieving professional competence.

This book, " **Redefining Organisational Excellence,**" draws on firsthand experience from high-performance operations to deliver vital leadership lessons as well as clear, accessible, and practical insights on managing teams in any corporate setting. This book provides a new and fascinating viewpoint on the factors that influence team and organisational greatness.

Today, business psychologists and other social scientists have a variety of perspectives on this topic. One evident flaw in the argument is the division between those who prioritise individual development and those who focus on cultural and organisational transformation. I will give you a variety of ideas on how to foster organisational excellence in this book. This allows individuals who prioritise organisational practise reform and those who highlight individual skills to communicate with one another, and invites readers to explore the reasons for both perspectives, or a hybrid of the two. The aim is to think about how these two opposing perspectives might be harmonised, or at the very least coordinated, to benefit both individuals and organisations as a whole. The central argument is that quality may be cultivated without jeopardising equity, which are both important elements of a democratic organisation.

The problems raised in this book have ramifications and importance in the domains of organisational psychology, practises and culture, organisational excellence philosophy, and organisational leadership. The book also examines organisations' aim to create a dynamic and happy working atmosphere in order to avoid unproductive or disruptive forces and ensure increased performance over time. Corporate employees, as well as scholars and practitioners of the subject, will find the book useful. This book, **"Redefining Organisational Excellence,"** lays out a structure for managers or leaders to follow in order to increase organisation performance in all sorts of businesses.

- Dr. Amit Das, Motivational Speaker, Leadership
Coach , Counsellor, and Mentor.

Acknowledgements

At the outset, I will thank my family for supporting me throughout the journey of writing my book and encouraging me to live my dreams; my son has always been instrumental in giving his inspiration to complete the writing of this book. Despite the fact that I am listed as the author of this book, ***"Redefining Organisational Excellence,"*** *would not have been published if I had depended entirely on my own talents. Creating this book required more than anything—it took a family of dedicated and caring people who were always prepared to lend a hand.*

Writing a book while working full-time is no simple task, so I'd want to express my gratitude to my amazing coworkers who act as cheerleaders in equal measure. Thank you, too, to my students and clients for your patience and unflinching support while I worked on this book!

Thank you to everyone who has listened to me argue for doing everything you can to make your life, including your work life, more progressive. I appreciate everyone's assistance throughout the process. This book would not have been possible without each of you having had an impact on my life in some manner.

Lastly, I would like to thank all the people with whom I have been associated. You gave me power. I would like to thank Notion Press for publishing my book. Finally, thank you all for gifting your time to read this book.

I'd want to convey my heartfelt appreciation to the almighty God for bestowing his blessings and being so gracious.

CHAPTER ONE

Impact Of Sustainable Change Management on Organisational Excellence

"Excellence is an art won by training and habituation. We do not act rightly because we have virtue or excellence, but we would rather have those things because we have acted rightly. We are what we repeatedly do. Excellence, then, is not an act but a habit." -Aristotle

Excellence, like so many adjectives in the English language today, is frequently hijacked in business contexts to be identical with a desired objective, such as perfection. True, excellence is connected to perfection in its most basic sense, but the two are not synonymous.

"Perfection is defined as being free of flaws or defects; faultless."

According to Psychology Today, perfectionism in the workplace may be the ultimate self-defeating tendency. It makes people slaves to achievement while keeping them fixated on failure, dooming them to a lifetime of doubt and unhappiness. It also has the unintended consequence of weakening accomplishment in the modern world.

"In a world that changing really quickly, the only strategy that is guaranteed to fail is not taking risks."
-Mark Zuckerberg

When organisation executives pursue or expect excellence in their business, whether on purpose or not, it is sometimes regarded by the ranks as perfection. One source of this misperception is the plethora of Power Point presentations that describe what is necessary in order to achieve greatness but seldom reveal how. Only the quality of the output and the frequent target of strikes are presented, and it is up to the ranks to figure out how.

For several decades, pursuing excellence in all organisation operations and processes has been a core corporate goal. Corporate planners associate excellence with increased productivity, lower costs, and increased profitability. Excellent organisations, it is often assumed, can weather economic changes, market shifts, and human attrition efficiently (with minimal harm). While the COVID-19 pandemic has not spared the largest conglomerates in terms of financial setbacks, it has prompted several well-run companies to reflect, recalibrate, and reinvent to fit into a changed world scenario in which excellence may well prove the all-important differentiator between successfully weathering economic upheaval and simply surviving.

This is because, while other organisations were downsizing, reorganising, and accepting reduced revenues and margins in 2020, great enterprises were considered to have defied the trend and, in reality, to have effectively exploited the crisis as a chance to advance. This has revived the discussion about the value of pursuing excellence as a meaningful, desirable objective connected with the organisation's long-term mission.

"To achieve excellence in anything, first knowledge is the need; a vision based on whole knowledge helps to fix a broad ambition that always helps as driving force to move ahead in one's venture; with experience and ideas one makes strides by intelligent moves!"

Excellence, is anything different that confers exceptional worth and value, such as a performance benchmark. Excellence is something to aspire towards and is frequently recognised with prizes. Whereas perfection is fixed—it's either faultless or devoid of flaws and defects, or it isn't—excellence is a journey that is more dynamic in nature.

When casually approaching someone for the first time, the subject of "what do you do?" frequently arises. There are several directions in which that query may go. However, if their focus appears to be on the workplace, I usually respond, "I work with organisations that strive to be outstanding." They respond, "But aren't all organisations, in one way or another?" At that point, the conversation becomes more interesting.

I can tell with confidence that no, not all organisations are pursuing excellence after spending a few decades working in "organisational excellence." Many people simply don't want to work hard enough to improve. They seek a fast solution. Excellence demands more effort than a quick summary.

Excellence may be defined and assessed in terms of what, how, and by whom, establishing baselines for minimal standards while allowing for creative execution. Rather than a single aim to achieve, achieving greatness is a process to be followed. You may cultivate your own attitudes to perform with an attitude of excellence in all you do, whether or not it is a fundamental value of the organisation. The best part about working in an excellence mindset is that you can work within your comfort zone, apply creativity and innovation, and contribute to the organisation's success. This, in turn, results in occupational satisfaction and fulfilment.

"To achieve excellence, fundamental changes are required in business operations."

A good organisation, examines first to determine if the work output is satisfactory before trying for higher performance. This might be the overall industry standard or a standard that is only adequate to meet the set aim. For example, in the case of a product specification, it may be a needed parameter range, or in the case of a customer, the maximum time permitted for delivery, and so forth.

Every business should have a well-defined mission that is reflected in the corporate culture. For example, if your objective is to provide the finest customer service in your sector, everyone in your organisation should keep this in mind while they go about their everyday tasks. Leaders in your business may set a good example by acting in accordance with your organisation's cultural values. Good-to-great leaders grasp key realities when it comes to getting started. First, starting with who allows you to more quickly adjust to a rapidly changing reality. If people board your bus because they think it's going somewhere, you'll have a problem when you're 10 miles down the road and realise you need to change directions because the world has changed. However, if people board the bus mostly because of the other wonderful individuals on board, they'll be far faster and smarter in adjusting to changing circumstances.

How will you have a deeper understanding of the key drivers of organisational excellence?

Can you perform 50 push-ups in a row? Let's shoot for 55 this time and 100 in two months! And if you're who you say you are, give us more than 100 in two months because that's how we push the envelope here! When all three tasks are successfully completed, an environment for excellence is established in that gym because each and every member is very inspired to do their very best because that's the value that defines you. That's who you are. Know exactly how you are doing at the moment and where you want to be in the specified future, and push the limits of every actionable goal along the way. You must use the same logic in your businesses and organisations.

Is your workplace a place where employees feel at ease and encouraged to do their best? An uncomfortable workplace atmosphere may sap your employees' motivation, resulting in low morale and significant employees turnover. To make your employees feel appreciated, make sure your workplace has appropriate lighting, comfortable office furniture, decent ergonomics, and spaces for them to hang out on breaks without bothering their coworkers. Also, keep the office clean. However, keep in mind the social and environmental elements.

You should also evaluate each member of your team on a regular basis to ensure they are living up to the corporate ideals you have established. People don't want to get stronger in most of the companies here because no one rewards them for being strong or punishes them for being weak most of the time, no one defines exactly what being strong or weak means, and they don't know how much they are lifting and how much they should be lifting because everything is ambiguous. Their team leaders do not provide them with a vision worth striving for, nor do they establish practical targets in the middle. Everyone is completely befuddled and mired in mediocrity. In this way, your country's cycle of mediocrity is maintained, and you must break it.

"I really do encourage other manufacturers to bring electric cars to market. It's a good thing, and they to bring it to market and keep iterating and improving to make better and better electric cars, because that's what's going to result in humanity achieving a sustainable transport future. I wish it was growing faster than it is."- Elon Musk

Although CEOs and organisations can set the standard for excellence, it will never be met unless it is customised and implemented at every level of the organisation. You may discover the same thing in each of these dramatic, astonishing, good-to-great organisation transformations: there were no miracle moment. Instead, each organisation, its executives, and its workers were kept on track for the long haul by a down-to-earth, pragmatic, committed-to-excellence method — a framework. In each case, steady discipline triumphed over the short cure.

A well-developed corporate social responsibility programme, which is vital for every organisation that cares about its employees and its reputation in the community, includes an employee wellbeing effort. However, a wellbeing effort is more than just a wellness programme. Instead, it will address your people's health, social, community, professional, and financial requirements. A suitable benefits package, a comprehensive compensation scheme, and wellness activities are all factors to consider. To promote continued action, inducements, effective communication, and policies will all be employed.

The term "metamorphosis" refers to significant changes in the operations of a organisation or organisation. This includes employees, processes, and technology. These modifications allow organisations to compete more effectively, become more efficient, or implement a total strategy shift. Business transformations are large-scale adjustments that companies undergo in order to achieve more than incremental gains in terms of change and growth.

The assessment and alteration of management procedures and corporate structures can be regarded as organisational metamorphosis or transformation. An important practice in the business model is added or removed, which necessitates more integration into the business operations. Due to the frequent changes in the corporate environment, it is a critical strategy for survival and competitive advantage.

"Organisations, like humans, go through phases of development before becoming mature brands."

However, even organisations that have completed significant changes may not necessarily reap the full financial rewards of their work. As a result, we looked more closely at the various stages of a transformation's life cycle to see where value is lost and what organisations can do to retain it. According to the research, three key transformation activities are particularly predictive of value capture, and organisations that have completed successful transformations are more inclined to follow the exact methods that support them.

Nonetheless, the findings show that even effective organisational reforms fall short of their full potential. Respondents who reported success believe that their organisations received only 67% of the maximum financial benefits that their reforms could have brought. Respondents from all other organisations, on the other hand, claim to have captured an average of just 37% of the potential value. Similarly, many organisations might enhance their timing; even those that have completed successful transformations could have benefited from doing so. It might imply maximising the organisation's potential through unleashing the potential of employees, repurposing intellectual property and proprietary technologies, or becoming more efficient.

Business transformations are multi-year efforts that necessitate substantial changes to the changing organisation's core characteristics. Given the project's scale, breadth, and timeline, it requires leadership from the top—whether it's the CEO or the Board of Directors—to position the organisation for long-term success and development. Previously, these transitions took several years. Because of the necessity of these modifications and the help available, the timetables have been expedited.

"There is no one-size-fits-all solution to achieving organisational excellence; instead, a multi-channel strategy to enhance and optimise corporate performance is required."

Defining your Hedgehog Concept is a crucial step in the process of going from average to excellent. But comprehension and insight don't develop instantly—or even after a single off-site meeting. The good-to-great organisations took an average of four years to develop their hedgehog concepts. It was a cycle repeated over and over by the right people, infused with brutal facts and guided by the three circles. It was an inherently iterative process, consisting of piercing questions, vigorous debate, resolute action, and autopsies without blame.

"Good" is no longer sufficient. You must succeed if you want to thrive in the cutthroat atmosphere of today. An organisation must pay attention to every aspect of its operation in order to maximise the efficiency and effectiveness of all of its resources. We have learned from years of working with many businesses and through a variety of performance improvement techniques that must be handled for a organisation to succeed. These crucial components are referred to as "pillars of organisational greatness." By concentrating on controlling the pillars of the organisation, organisational excellence aims to transform the organisation over time. These organisational pillars are not novel on their own. Bringing them together and managing them as a team is the secret to organisational excellence.

What makes a corporate transformation successful?

Surprisingly, few studies have attempted to quantify what makes a corporate transition successful. I examined multiple global companies that had undergone transformation. I opined that transformation is more difficult than expected; successful companies shared a common focus on initiatives that prioritised employees, such as DIBE (Diversity, Inclusion, Belonging, and Equality) programs and support for women managers' careers, in addition to competitive pay and access to health care. Business transformation has long been seen as the holy grail of the business world—something that is constantly sought for yet impossible to achieve. When John Kotter made his now-famous statement that 70% of business transformation programs fail more than 25 years ago, he emphasised the problem. The latest McKinsey study on transitions reveals that success is elusive and requires a complete strategy.

However, some acts are more likely to lead to the realisation of the financial rewards at stake. The results of McKinsey's latest global survey, which builds on 15 years of original McKinsey research on organisational transformations, underscore an enduring truth: The more transformation activities a organisation performs, the better its prospects for success. However, success is the exception rather than the rule.

Despite the fact that you've known for years that a holistic approach to organisational transformation is more favorable to long-term change, the average success rate has remained stubbornly low. Less than a third of respondents (all of whom had been involved in a transformation in the previous five years) feel their organisations' transformations were effective in terms of both boosting organisational performance and sustaining those improvements over time. Setting effective and ambitious transformational goals is insufficient. People must comprehend what these goals imply in terms of their day-to-day occupations and what they will be required to accomplish differently. If they don't understand how they fit into the transformation, their behaviors and work processes will remain unchanged.

However, the survey findings imply that there may be a perception gap: top executives are approximately 20% more likely than other workers to perceive that their transformation goals have been modified for relevant employees across the organisation. The most successful organisations, according to the survey, are more likely to involve employees and engage them in face-to-face communication, specifically, line-manager briefings (cited by 65% of successful transformation respondents), leadership town halls, and a cascade of information throughout the business (for more on employee communication and engagement).

Every organisation can see transformation as a means of gaining a competitive advantage. In their field, companies with strong brands, good employees management, and ethical business practices will stand out. Because it comes with the territory, human resources is in a unique position to help others through organisational transformation. As you transition to a new organisational paradigm, use this information to help workers overcome their aversion to change.

Organisations that go from good to great don't have a label for their transition, and they don't have a program. They don't whine or complain about a crisis, and they don't create one when none exists. There is no evidence that money and change mastery are linked. And although fear does not motivate change, it does encourage mediocrity. Acquisitions can't spur greatness either; two mediocre companies don't make a great one. Technology is crucial, but it only comes into play after the transformation has already occurred. Finally, spectacular results do not come from dramatic processes—at least not if you want them to persist. A genuine revolution, one that feels like a revolution to the people who are experiencing it, is exceedingly unlikely to result in a long-term jump from excellent to exceptional.

Despite the trauma caused by the epidemic, many strong organisations retain their distinctive capabilities in industrial processes, strategic sourcing, and financial management. To get off to a good start in terms of excellence, they would need to promote it as a key cultural value inside their enterprises, much like a safety culture, equal opportunity, or gender equality.

What is the difficult element of driving excellence in your organisation?

The difficult element of driving excellence is that it demands shaking people out of their comfort zones (particularly those who have previously achieved the requisite outcomes) and allowing them to experiment with novel ideas. But, again, COVID has always been about ushering in a new normal. The coronavirus epidemic has opened up vistas of new methods of functioning successfully and inspired employees to be imaginative as well as optimise existing approaches.

Most good businesses would be okay with a top management specialist spearheading excellence initiatives. This will entail rethinking strategy, implementing new formats, brainstorming, training/retraining sessions, and so on. COVID, on the other hand, has seen organisational innovation evolve from the ground up, and the time may be perfect to return to making this attempt a ground-level activity that penetrates the layers. Much like the Japanese automakers of the 1970s and 1980s, who pioneered groundbreaking shop floor programmes that substantially enhanced efficiency and set new norms of manufacturing excellence, Consistency is what elevates a mediocre performance to the level of brilliance.

When the strength of human tenacity is paired with the necessary knowledge and skill set, the recipe for success in terms of greatness is delivered. Even MNCs that faced existential crises as a result of the pandemic did a deep dive to re-evaluate their fundamental competencies and encouraged workers at all levels to think outside the box in order to sustain morale and seek new meanings for their different positions within the organisation.

Switching to new business or operational models is one example of a broad and strategic scope. Business transformations are carried out in order to provide value to a organisation. By implementing business transformation basics into their organisations and the products they supervise, product management can act as an inspiration, a testing ground, and a momentum-maintaining cheerleader for bringing these ideas into reality.

It is generally observed that organisations and workforces that persevered in the face of adversity, learned new skills, and communicated with one another on a regular basis not only survived the worst of the pandemic, but also created substantial value that has the potential to last in the long run. Workforces infused with (or who imbibed) the fundamental philosophy of constancy of excellent performance set the standard for their particular enterprises.

Whether it was a procurement department that, despite material availability, economic uncertainty, and logistics issues, bought cost-effectively on a regular basis, adding considerably to the value chain. Alternatively, a quality assurance department with fewer people might still ensure that consistently high quality standards are maintained at the lowest possible cost. Client-centricity has recovered the spotlight as part of excellence initiatives, with organisations understanding that in difficult circumstances, customers seek regular providers to work closely with them and for out-of-the-box solutions that ensure cost advantages on both sides in cash-strapped times.

COVID has emphatically stated that the employee is still the most crucial gear in the organisational wheel and the focal point of all excellence initiatives. While technology and automation have taken the shine off of organisational growth in recent years, the focus is now, and properly so, on human resources. Companies' HR functions have quickly rebalanced to become people-centric again, rather than system-centric in the past. All of this raises the fundamental question of excellence, stemming from the intrinsic human drive for perfection and for doing things correctly.

As the old adage says, "If an activity is worth performing, it is worth doing well."

The innovative thinking that goes into the produced items might be equally as important as the inventive thinking that goes into the organisation's operations. Any established organisation that wants to maximise performance, increase efficiency, and stay in business in five or ten years should look into business transformation options. There will always be areas, procedures, and structures that might be improved, and ignoring these improvements in favor of the status quo is often short-sighted and harmful. Business transformation may be many things when it has a broad reach. There are several ways to categorise business transformation activities, but they usually fall into one or more of the categories.

This transformation is concerned with the "how" of completing tasks and may involve agile transformation. It usually entails a lot of process improvement and automation in order to focus on higher-value tasks. This is usually a continuous endeavor, beginning with the more prevalent ways and progressing to those with lower returns. The ultimate objective is to free the corporation from these responsibilities so that it may innovate or deliver higher-value services and products to the market. Information, data, and digital transformations—focusing these transformations on leveraging technology to generate more value is the focus. It might come in the form of new, more efficient ways of gathering and exchanging data such as a digital CRM system or online ordering. It also includes harnessing technology and data to deliver new goods and services in the end, both by using technology to develop, produce, and distribute them more quickly and by incorporating digital assets into the new offers themselves.

Long ago, there was a story about a Japanese baseball club team travelling the American continent. The squad journeyed from city to city, playing a series of matches, losing more than they won against talented American club sides. One feature of the Japanese team's behaviour, however, stood out and was consistent throughout the tour. When the Japanese team finished a game and it was time to leave the stadium, they would willingly take 10 minutes off to clean their dressing room — lockers, tables, drawers, benches — to restore it to the exact perfect form in which they walked in earlier in the day. A curious scribe asked the squad the purpose of this behaviour near the conclusion of their journey. The squad members were noticeably surprised that such a question had been posed in the first place, and their reaction was, "Someone took the time to make us comfortable by providing us with a spick-and-span changing room." The very least we can do is repay the favour. It was the most natural thing in the world for them to clean up (and clean up properly!) after usage, and to do so with the same attention and commitment that they put into their game. Let us strive to make greatness a habit that will sustain companies in difficult times.

Many changes rely on changing resource allocation. Organisational change begins with an assessment of how to staff various departments as well as the structure of those divisions. Organisations can find possibilities by looking at in-house talents and expertise, how employees are employed, and the various reporting systems. These possibilities might indicate a need to simplify or expand in order to attain more development and success. Breaking down silos, flattening the organisation, and right-sizing the headcount are all possible goals. Top-down bureaucratic hierarchies aren't always the greatest for supporting speedy decision-making and adapting to new events as organisations strive for growth in competitive marketplaces. While changing the management structure (removing middlemen, etc.) is a part of the answer, enabling individuals to make their own decisions or swiftly find a consensus is considerably more important. This necessitates knowledge sharing and socialising as well as the establishment of clear communication routes and general organisational openness.

Organisational excellence requires trust. Establish trust among all members of your business, from entry-level employees to senior managers. Encourage your employees to express their issues openly so that they may be handled as soon as possible. Nothing builds trust more effectively than clear communication followed by fast and deliberate action. Allow your employees to take action without seeking assistance or direction from their managers. To encourage this proactive behaviour, ensure that all of your employees have the resources they need to address problems, like access to client records or the ability to use modest amounts of organisation assets without seeking permission. Also, ensure that your policies promote empowerment. By actively encouraging workers to participate in choices that affect their work, you can instil confidence in them and demonstrate that they are valuable parts of your business.

Professionally, give chances for your employees to strive for excellence in their work. However, give them the opportunity for personal development as well. Good examples include assisting people in developing better money management, parenting, and community service abilities. Providing chances for your employees to acquire new professional and personal skills may boost retention and productivity, allowing you to keep a more highly trained and motivated team.

It would almost be impolite not to include Google in a list of organisations with a strong culture. For years, Google has been associated with culture, and it has set the standard for many of the perks and privileges that startups are now recognised for. Free meals, staff vacations and parties, cash bonuses, open lectures by high-level executives, gyms, a dog-friendly atmosphere, and other benefits are available. Google employees are regarded as being ambitious, talented, and among the finest in the industry. Maintaining a consistent culture throughout Google's headquarters and satellite offices, as well as among the many departments inside the organisation, has proven difficult as the organisation has grown and spread out. The greater a organisation grows, the more its culture must evolve to accommodate more people.

The more a organisation grows, the more its culture must evolve to meet the increased number of people and the demand for management. While Google continues to receive high marks for compensation, benefits, and promotion, some employees have noted the growing pains that come with such a large organisation, such as the stress that comes with working in a competitive atmosphere. If organisation culture doesn't allow for a proper work-life balance, hiring and demanding the best from people may quickly become a source of stress. Like Google, Facebook is a organisation that has experienced explosive growth while also being associated with a distinct corporate culture.

Many similar organisations, including Facebook, provide a lot of food, stock options, open office space, on-site laundry, a focus on cooperation and open communication, a competitive environment that stimulates personal growth and learning, and outstanding perks. Facebook, like other organisations, has the same challenges: a highly competitive market leads to a stressful and competitive workplace. Furthermore, a loose and organic organisational structure that works well for a smaller organisation does not function well for a bigger one.

"It is impossible to escape the impression that people commonly use false standards of measurement — that they seek power, success and wealth for themselves and admire them in others, and that they underestimate what is of true value in life." — Sigmund Freud

Whatever a small business appears to be on paper in the beginning, the leader or founder might be the most intriguing element of that organisation, which no one supporting them should ever take for granted. Solution providers trying to force their views, thoughts, and attitudes on a organisation is something I have seen far too frequently as a client and now as a consulting partner. Of course, that solution provider was selected for their competence, but not at the expense of the organisation or the leader's culture.

Even if things are a little bumpy within the organisation, it is always crucial to study and watch how it all began and how it is surviving with the person who was there from the beginning. If you believe the culture needs to change, whether at the request of the leader or because you've noticed enough to talk about it, you must construct the other three components alongside that change, not separately from it. If one isn't viable (for example, new technology investments), you'll have to put in more effort into people or processes to overcome it. You are convinced that the combination of leadership, strategy, customers, measurements, workforce, operations, and results will get you there.

It is critical for every organisation to keep its employees motivated and engaged. Employees can be motivated in a variety of ways since everyone has different goals, but the organisational values and culture are the ultimate motivators for all employees. It's a simple question with a simple response. When an organisation's basic principles are clear, its employees know who they are and what they are a part of. Employees will be motivated to join and work for a organisation that shares their personal fundamental beliefs. These people will put in more effort because they are passionate about what they are doing and for whom they are doing it.

Leaders and teams that want to see their organisations succeed must refocus their efforts and reevaluate their goals as rapidly as possible, going from being "simple generators of products or services" to "value deliverers" for their customers and other stakeholders. This transition necessitates a mentality motivated by a shared corporate purpose, which should be backed up by an ever-improving management system. The main issue with industries is the high rate of turnover and the high expectations that employees have for their careers.

Having a high-performing workforce is conducive to business success. Strong, shared values transform an organisation into a hologram in which each component holds enough information to convey the entire organisation in a condensed form. By monitoring one person, whether it's a manufacturing worker, a front-desk receptionist, or a senior manager, an observer may gain insight into the whole organisation's culture and ways of conducting business.

Understanding your organisation's mission is the first step in building an effective organisation. Once this is accomplished, you will be able to more clearly define your long-term objectives. Following that, objectives that will assist you in moving toward your goals might be developed. These objectives can then be allocated to people inside the organisation so that each one is completed by a specific person or team of people. This responsibility is critical to ensure that your organisation's plan is implemented. The importance of information is crucial to the success of any modern organisation and cannot be overstated. Develop metrics that will allow you to track the effectiveness of all aspects of your business and discover strategies to monitor them. For example, you may request that your marketing department measure their monthly website visitor increase in Google Analytics so you can evaluate how successfully their efforts are driving visitors to your site. Most significantly, you may monitor progress toward the goals outlined in "Strategic Direction" above. It is vital to note that in order to have a balanced approach to performance, your measurements should be evenly focused on sales, operations, and people or culture.

Facebook has established conference rooms in different buildings, plenty of outside roaming areas for breaks, and managers including CEO Mark Zuckerberg working in the open office space with other employees to tackle these problems. It's an attempt to create a flat organisational culture by promoting equality among competitors through the use of buildings and space.

Adobe is a corporation that goes out of its way to give its workers difficult assignments and then gives them the trust and support they need to succeed. Adobe goods are linked with creativity, and the individuals who make them can only be fully free to create if they are not micromanaged.

While Adobe offers the same advantages and privileges as any other modern creative organisation, its culture rejects micromanagement in favor of trusting people to achieve their best. Adobe, for example, does not utilise ratings to determine staff skills since it believes that this restricts innovation and negatively impacts teamwork. More than anything, managers take on the role of coach, allowing employees to create goals and decide how they should be evaluated. Employees are often offered stock options so that they feel they have a share in the organisation's success and may benefit from it. Adobe's open workplace culture includes ongoing training and a culture that encourages risk-taking without fear of repercussions.

Many of these businesses have comparable perks and bonuses, but these do not entirely determine the culture. The way employees are treated, as well as the amount of ownership and trust they are given, is an important aspect of business culture. One word of caution: concentrating solely on business culture at the expense of other workforce issues (safety, rules, regulations) might lead to abuses or create uncomfortable circumstances for employees. Even the strongest cultural examples on this list have critics. Always keep in mind that the finest culture makes all employees feel safe and welcome, never isolated or uneasy. Focusing solely on "cultural fit" makes it tough to acquire and welcome workers who aren't part of the organisation's current culture, even if they'd be a valuable addition and fantastic counterweight. If your corporate culture is causing you to have a homogenised staff that thinks and acts the same way, it has to be changed.

"The excellence and inspiration of truth is in the pursuit, not in the mere having of it. The pursuit of all truth is a kind of gymnastics; a man swings from one truth with higher strength to gain another. The continual glory is the possibility opening before us." -Edwin Hubbel Chapin

Mergers and acquisitions did not lead to success. There was no press release, announcement, rollout, or anything to promote good-to-great transformations. Rather, they were the consequence of persistent, tenacious efforts that appeared totally ordinary—even boring—to onlookers both inside and outside the organisation. The industry didn't matter: Some good-to-great organisations focused on unglamorous sectors and nevertheless managed to create excellent outcomes. Every corporation seeks organisational excellence, yet many business executives are unable to identify how to accomplish it. It has always been remarked that "change is a constant in business," but this is especially true now from a marketing standpoint with the increase in digital transformation projects

How can a organisation become a fantastic place to work?

Many organisations aspire to this, but few have a clear understanding of the effort required to make it a reality. HR strategy has been very basic for the previous five years: build an environment where people want to work. It's a lot simpler to say than to accomplish. Making the required adjustments requires a lot of effort and dedication, and it may be unpleasant. In a recent piece, the author emphasised the importance of taking the time to map out the organisation's intended culture as a cornerstone to becoming a wonderful place to work. These are the four key areas to focus on as part of your journey to creating a great workplace.

In a corporate setting, what does organisational change imply? Organisational transformation (ORG) is a strategic method of getting your organisation from where it is now to where it needs to be in the future, according to ORG. In many circumstances, this transition is necessary to address a long-overdue problem or change. Enhancing the adaptability, agility, and efficacy of organisational processes and workflows.

Organisational transformation aligns with business goals and can aim at a variety of things, including: Digital transformation, for example, entails keeping up with and being at the forefront of technology advancements. By lowering the time and expense of executing activities, any organisation may gain a competitive edge by implementing and employing the correct technology. The capacity to be nimble and sensitive to industry, technology, and workforce trends, as well as pivot when necessary, is required while transforming a business. To move everyone from point A to point B while embracing key principles that make it distinctive, the corporate culture must be adaptive.

"Those who lead by example and demonstrate passion for what they do make it much easier for their followers to do the same." --Marshall Goldsmith

For instance, an organisation may discover that it has a reputation for high employee turnover as a result of unmanageable workloads. Rather than allowing this pattern to continue, the leadership team and human resources team decide to embark on an organisational transformation process that includes a complete overhaul of all job roles as well as the implementation of new technology to streamline tasks. The united effort makes the organisation more successful and productive, as well as a better environment for workers to work in. For a variety of reasons, organisational transformation is essential. It is inextricably linked to organisational success and, as a result, to business outcomes. Because every business goes through cycles of development and change, now is a good time to assess how the organisation is performing and develop a strategic plan for the future. The following are some of the important areas that organisational change has an influence on: How effective are your organisation's antiquated hierarchy and processes? This is frequently the area of business that requires the greatest reform in order for the organisation to reach its full potential.

According to a Deloitte study, "53% of leaders feel that transitioning to team-based working has resulted in considerable performance improvement." An organisation where all employees work their jobs for the organisation's overall development must realise one thing: they are a professional family, and they must support each other with whatever problems they experience in their departments. That may happen when a corporation begins to celebrate each employee's accomplishments in order to make them feel like a family. This type of improvement has the potential to improve official settings. Not just the office atmosphere, but every employee must put in some effort to make their workplace a better place for everyone. It is not uncommon for some workers to neglect to execute their jobs and attempt to cause issues for others. This type of employee conduct breeds negativity in them, which might exacerbate the situation at work, leading to him or her being dismissed from his or her position.

Many corporate executives are considering organisational change. Managers that are on top of their game are continually seeking ways to improve their organisation's efficiency and culture. This work is especially important at times of transition, such as the one we've been through as a result of the epidemic. It's also at this point that organisational reform becomes a determinant of long-term viability. Organisational transformation strategies can provide your organisation with continuity and opportunity at the crossroads between stagnation and sustainability. Any sort of transformation has an impact on your staff first and foremost. As a result, HR plays a critical part in the process.

Most organisations want their workers or employers to back them up in their organisational decisions. And it is common for some employees or employers to disagree with the organisation's choice. Instead of responding irrationally, those employees might consider making a decision that will benefit each of them in the long run. Instead of behaving irrationally, those workers may think about making a decision that will help each of them in their greatest career, and while there may be some troubles along the way, it will eventually be over.

Organisations frequently endure leadership changes and departmental adjustments, and hierarchies are dismantled. A specific change action is carried out, with role models, specialists, and mentors on hand to guide staff in the right direction. In this stage, training for new ideas and technology is common, pushing everyone to learn new concepts and take a step into the future.

What does a successful organisational change entail? Kurt Lewin, a German-American psychologist, developed the basic Change Management Model, which defines three stages of organisational transformation that promote success. During the unfreezing stage leadership generates the notion that change is required to better the organisation at this point. This may be accomplished in two ways:

(1) Recognising the need for change, and

(2) Encouraging new behaviors to replace old ones.

Human resources are critical at this phase in finding and communicating data signs of transformative need. Low employee satisfaction and excessive turnover, for example, may indicate a need for cultural change. This drives change based on profitability and productivity when it is supported by management. Adapting At this point, the organisation has overcome any resistance to reform. Old undesirable behaviors are replaced by new desired actions.

A successful organisation must recognise that innovative product ideas may be the key to its success. These novel concepts have the potential to transform the commercial market. Eventually, all of the organisation's workers begin to feel safe in their assigned departmental responsibilities. As a result, a corporation should be open to new ideas for the organisation's and its employees' overall development.

Working in a organisation may appear to be a difficult task at first, but if an employee attempts to grasp his or her responsibilities, it will no longer be so difficult. For several reasons, the working atmosphere in the office might change from day to day. To avoid this, all employees must be honest and disciplined in their assigned duties.

Once you've set your strategic direction and determined how you'll assess progress, you'll need to make sure that critical messages are communicated throughout your business. Consider your plan for expressing your values and expectations to individuals at all levels of your organisation. Email? What about meetings and training sessions? Or how about disseminating information via the workplace intranet? To reach everyone, you may need to employ a combination of these strategies. Whatever communication medium you employ, keep in mind that communication should always be two-way. Allow your employees to provide feedback on business policies and discuss suggestions for change. Indeed, encouraging grass-roots communication is critical.

"Effective grassroots communications enable problems to be handled efficiently at the lowest possible level, rather than escalating up the management levels."

Most employees may not be involved in each other's work at times, but when a critical moment occurs in the department, they must help one another, and this support should be recognised as part of the organisation's goodwill. While strong rivalry among employees may foster a healthy spirit among all employees, certain employees may attempt to share their political expertise in the workplace. Some workers play politics between the employer and the employee in order to create some sort of misunderstanding between them, with the employee eventually benefiting from the corporate politics. Such office politics may wreak havoc on a pleasant working atmosphere. Employees in most companies face some form of communication gap with their bosses as a result of their position or attitude.

As a result, that might be a probable cause of the organisation's imbalance, in which all employees are negative about their workplace. And, in order to avoid such negativity, an employer must remember that all of the organisation's employees are equal in terms of service delivery. Each organisation employee has their own career goals, which may range from person to person.

Some employees have higher expectations for their careers, and they work extra hard in their departments to achieve them. As a result, this type of hard work or analysis of superior job ability may help an employee plan his or her future growth in the organisation. And this might result in an external force that appears to be beneficial to their career.

Many businesses do not value diversity in their workplaces or departments. It's also likely that the majority of their coworkers disagree with their authority as women. When employers learn their higher authority bearer is a woman or a lady, they may ask candidates about their point of view during interviews. This type of gender discrimination might contribute to a negative atmosphere in the workplace.

A workplace should be a location where a person may be inspired to contribute their talents and abilities to the organisation's overall development as well as their own professional development. It is a place where an employee and an employer collaborate to improve their professional pleasure. It's possible that a person working in a hostile workplace will have difficulty fulfilling his or her obligations and responsibilities. According to the me, "a happy employee is more likely to be innovative and productive." Furthermore, happy employees are a valuable asset to any organisation. As a result, it is critical for businesses to make their employees happy.

Organisational productivity is influenced by the work environment. Building a better place to work is closely tied to having a pleasant work environment. Employees are more likely to perform effectively in a better environment, which aids the organisation's success. The key question is, "What makes an organisation a wonderful place to work?" and it is likely to be a very subjective one. A variety of elements influence whether an individual finds a place "excellent" or not, including monetary pay, senior appreciation, infrastructure, interesting professional prospects, appropriate career growth, awards and recognition, as well as team support.

It is critical to comprehend what makes your organisation a fantastic place to work and how to improve it. The following are some of the factors that contribute to or assist in establishing a pleasant working environment for both employees and employers.

- It's important to have a clear vision and goal.
- Critical Communication that works.
- Employees are allowed to grow in a "flexible" manner.
- It encourages meritocracy.
- Having a culture of collaboration.
- Leadership advice that is easily accessible.
- Stay away from politics.
- Employees' candid feedback is sought.
- Leadership that is both honest and impartial.
- A more favourable working environment.
- Employees who are passionate and devoted.
- Encourage openness and transparency.
- It also assists in the development of management skills.
- Providing incentives and expressing gratitude.
- Keep only what you require in your immediate vicinity.

- Maintain a clean work environment in order to avoid neck and back pain.
- Keeping plants, air fresheners, open windows.
- Keep a supply of water and snacks on hand.
- Natural Light and Open Windows for proper brightness and lighting.
- Small victories are celebrated.
- Maintain a comfortable office temperature.
- The hours of employment are flexible.
- Options for working from home.
- Time off is paid indefinitely.
- Financials that are open and transparent.
- Promotions that are not prejudiced.
- Equal acclaim and rewards.
- Tasks are distributed evenly.
- Feedback that is both frequent and open.
- Performance evaluations are both positive and negative.
- Encourage employees to do work that they enjoy, since this will help them advance professionally.

You've been given a list of distinctive characteristics that distinguish a organisation as a great place to work so you can see them throughout your job hunt. It is critical to make an employer feel good about his or her working environment, and in order to do so, an employer must begin encouraging employees in his or her office to perform more effectively.

As a result, it is critical to motivate organisation employees with some type of professional encouragement, such as promotions or performance recognition. All of these factors contribute to an employee's feeling good or fantastic about their job. A organisation is a place where all employees and their bosses collaborate and responsibly carry out their responsibilities. It's feasible that this task delivery will profit if they strive to learn from one another.

There may have been instances where an employer acted maturely in handling a critical circumstance, and these experiences may all assist an employee learn from his or her employer in the future. Working in a positive atmosphere may necessitate some degree of optimism among employees and employers, but the fact is that this may be achieved by encouraging healthy competition among these companies and their employees to do better in their jobs. These contests may be introduced in order to establish a realistic aim for the financial year-end competition. This type of competition is frequently performed in the marketing or sales departments to motivate employees. There is a frequent type of error that most employees make when working in the workplace. For example, an employee exclusively talks with his or her coworkers in his or her department and never seeks contact with anybody else in the department. This type of behaviour might severely limit the options available to the employee.

As a result, if an employee tries to mix or communicate with other office employees members, there is a chance that the employee may wind up with a large number of coworkers. Some companies provide entertaining acts or events in the office on special occasions.

For a successful completion, it is also recommended that all of the organisation's workers participate in such activities, either as participants or as volunteers. As a result, all of these efforts may help to create a climate that allows all of the organisation's employees to feel more at ease in their workplace. If an employer or employee wants to feel good about their job, there is a simple thing they can do to maintain a healthy working relationship. It's possible that a junior employer starts denigrating a senior employee for no apparent reason, and this creates a negative environment for both corporate employees.

As a result, in order to avoid such conflict between workers, an employer must speak with them in order to address issues and establish a positive work environment for their own good. It is normal in any organisation for most workers or employers to demand some type of performance appreciation from their superiors in order to improve their department's performance. As a result, in order to meet such goals in the workplace, higher-ups must consider employees performance evaluations in order to motivate and improve their department's performance. To make a organisation a place where all of the workers enjoy working together, an employer must create an image that allows other employees to express gratitude for the assistance they have received in the workplace.

Do you look forward to another amazing day at work when you wake up every morning, or do they drag yourselves to work every day?

Managing a positive work environment is essential for maximising employee productivity. Working people nowadays spend about a third of their lives at work, with a significant portion of their productive lives committed to their organisations.

Now, you've developed a strong value system in which we aim to establish a trusting connection with our employees in order to make the organisation seem more like a family. The primary components on which you build your human resource techniques are dialogue, feedback, communication, and trust, and these values constitute the core of our high-performance culture. Each employee is a precious human resource who must be nourished, cultivated, and valued. Human resources, unlike stocks, money, and other inanimate resources, are not replaceable. Individual training requires time and effort, and changing people at whim is neither easy nor in the best interests of the organisation.

As a result, each organisation's primary value should be respect for its people. If you treat your employees with dignity and respect as a manager, they will immediately reciprocate to the organisation. Respect your subordinates, communicate with them, listen to their ideas, implement their suggestions, and make them feel appreciated. This method not only helps employees feel appreciated, but it also provides us with a release valve for any pent-up tension or feelings. The pattern and means of working in an organisation change as the times change.

Is your organisation a monolith when it comes to people, or does it have a varied workforce in terms of gender, linguistics, racial, ethnic, and religious backgrounds?

Young and inexperienced leaders, in particular, are continuously in need of direction and mentorship from more experienced executives. Experience reveals that diverse organisations with a diversified workforce (gender, linguistic, racial, ethnic, and religious) are more open to new ideas because they are exposed to a wider range of viewpoints and have a more flexible cognitive process. It will always be a rewarding place to work at an organisation where employees support and aid one another at all times rather than engage in cutthroat rivalry. Employees who are always competing with one another foster office politics and degrade the workplace atmosphere. Being a part of social activities gives workers, especially the younger ones, a sense of increased purpose and usefulness. Involving workers in the organisation's beneficial social activities gives them another reason to stay with the organisation.

A great place to work values and supports its workers while also pushing them to advance within the organisation. Managers and workers at these organisations have a mutual trust and regard for one another, as well as a shared dedication to individual and corporate success. Great organisations make an effort to address the financial, mental, physical, and emotional requirements of their employees. Employees are more productive, pleased, and eager to stay at the organisation for the long haul as a consequence.

A great place to work values and supports its workers while also pushing them to advance within the organisation. Managers and workers at these organisations have a mutual trust and regard for one another, as well as a shared dedication to individual and corporate success. Great organisations make an effort to address the financial, mental, physical, and emotional requirements of their employees. Employees are more productive, pleased, and eager to stay at the organisation for the long haul as a consequence.

To relieve stress from office work and responsibilities, a organisation might organise a stress reliever activity for its employees, and some organisations do so to help their employees feel more at ease in the workplace. It's possible that the majority of companies that utilise such stress relievers have the highest rate of excellent workers in their offices.

As a result, it is critical to comprehend the importance of such stress-relieving activities. In every business, time management is critical. And this should be strictly followed in all businesses. It is vital to have such time-management skills in the workplace. Some organisations follow rigorous restrictions in the name of time management, and they put their employees on such a tight schedule that they wind up dealing with unfavourable conditions at work.

For the sake of the organisation's wellbeing, an organisation must implement a fair time management method to minimise such strain. An employee who is new to his or her workplace and worried about his or her responsibilities, for example, may be uneasy being around such highly competent colleagues. At that point, he or she must make an impression as a nice person, which can only be accomplished by his or her ability to impress all members of the workforce. This first impression of his or her personality might either help or hurt him or her at work.

"Working for a good employer is enjoyable, gratifying, and challenging. While job hunting, look for organisations with happy employees, attractive perks, and a healthy corporate culture. These are all indicators of a fantastic place to work."

According to a study on corporate social responsibility conducted in 2020, as many as 67% of those polled chose to work for socially responsible businesses. It's critical to have employees that are educated to support each other rather than pull the rug out from under each other.

Employees in innovative organisations are encouraged to take chances, exchange ideas, and provide suggestions. As a consequence, employees are more motivated and proud of their job as a consequence, and the organisation has more opportunities to expand and flourish as a result. They look for an organisation that values open lines of communication and takes employee feedback into account when making decisions. Working for a organisation that is continually developing new products, strategies, and procedures may be a thrilling experience. They look for an organisation that is a market leader and where employees feel comfortable discussing their thoughts with management. Employees that are invested and interested in the outcome of their job are commonly found in great organisations. They are committed to the organisation's objective and strive toward common goals that go beyond sales and earnings. Furthermore, the organisation's leadership is interested in and engaged in the day-to-day operations of the organisation, and they are attentive to queries and suggestions.

Working for an organisation is likely to be a terrific place to work if it is a dream job for the majority of individuals in your sector. Look for organisations with strong brands and competitive pricing. Check to see whether a organisation has received any awards for the best workplace in your sector or region. Talented employees are drawn to great organisations, and they often remain for a long time. Employees' trust and dedication to addressing problems and accomplishing goals may be earned by companies that are upfront about their challenges, accomplishments, and everyday operations. Meetings or briefings on the organisation's issues and triumphs on a regular basis. Open-book management refers to a management style in which the organisation's executives disclose financial and other key information to all employees. When confronted with financial, operational, or strategic issues, leaders who solicit employee comments or suggestions are more likely to succeed.

Everyone's viewpoint matters in a transparent workplace, and everyone shares in the organisation's success. Employees like to work with leaders that are confident, effective, and fair. Good leadership not only keeps people engaged, motivated, and goal-oriented, but it also helps organisations prosper financially. Managers that treat their employees like adults encourage them to make decisions and work on their own. They also value their employees, solicit feedback, and reward them for their hard work and good contributions. Because mobile phones make communication so easy, employees are now expected to be available 24 hours a day, seven days a week, whether it's Saturday or Sunday. This kind of adaptability should not only be expected of students, but also encouraged.

As a result, stringent log-in times may be replaced with flexi hours, and employees can be granted a few days of work from home to offer them a more comfortable and accommodating atmosphere. This is critical in order to retain competent and experienced employees, particularly women, who may want more professional flexibility in order to balance the demands of parenting. Furthermore, according to a recent poll on workplace flexibility conducted by HR service provider Randstad, up to 53% of Indian respondents favour telecommuting. As a manager, you must ensure that an employee's contributions to your organisation are never overlooked. Praise should be freely given in your organisation; this motivates employees and makes them feel valued.

While performance gaps and mismanagement must be identified and remedied, managers should prioritise delivering solutions rather than simply blaming individuals. Even after putting their all into a project, a team may not be able to achieve the anticipated outcomes. As a manager, your strategy should be to review each completed project for flaws and errors, and then teach your employees improved execution techniques. Great places to work have employees with different levels of expertise, backgrounds, and beliefs. They recognise the importance of having a diverse employees and make an effort to employ a diverse group of people. A diverse workforce is more likely to generate intriguing ideas and innovative solutions. A diverse workplace is also friendly to new employees and encourages morale among existing ones.

How can leaders and human resource experts assist in the change of an organisation?

Human resources plays a key role in preserving clarity, conveying change, and dealing with any opposition. The organisational transformation process is complete after the changes have settled and become the norm. Changes in behavior are integrated with a new set of values and expectations by all leaders and workers.

"Managers and human resources collaborate to help workers who are having problems. The new organisation appears to have a promising future."

According to research, leaders and HR play a critical role in fostering long-term transformation. 80% of HR practitioners agree that top or senior management is required for successful organisational change. Transformation does not occur in a vacuum. Instead, it must be a comprehensive strategy that covers several aspects of the business in order to be effective. For example, if your objective is to alter your processes to make them more agile and collaborative, you'll need to think about how it will affect your organisational structure, the technology you're using, and whether or not there will be a skills gap.

When going through organisational transformation, Genuity employed this strategy to acknowledge the job done, the reason why the work was done, and the meaning of the work for each employee. Make a list of the steps you'll need to take to alter the organisation. Begin with the end-results in mind and work your way back through the organisation. The transformation process is made easier with a strategy that includes a timeframe. A strategy with a schedule helps to make the transformation process more real and keeps the focus on the task at hand.

"Transformation does not occur in a vacuum. Instead, it must be a comprehensive strategy that covers several aspects of the business in order to be effective."

For example, if your objective is to alter your processes to make them more agile and collaborative, you'll need to think about how it will affect your organisational structure, the technology you're using, and whether or not there will be a skills gap. When going through organisational transformation, genuity employed this strategy to acknowledge the job done, the reason why the work was done, and the meaning of the work for each employee. Make a list of the steps you'll need to take to alter the organisation. Begin with the end-results in mind and work your way back through the organisation. The transformation process becomes more real with a strategy that includes a schedule, which aids in keeping the process on track.

Let's imagine you want to increase your employee experience, performance, and productivity by X% by switching from obsolete workplace technologies to more current, efficient platforms. Preliminary tool research, vendor demos, selecting and purchasing the correct tool, integrating it, and onboarding your workers to utilize it would all be part of your timelined strategy. It's difficult to make all of the necessary changes all at once. Instead, prioritise the issues you wish to address first, such as deploying three new workplace technologies one by one rather than all at once.

"I believe you have to be willing to be misunderstood if you're going to innovate." --Jeff Bezos

It's also possible that the transformation strategy will evolve over time. Reevaluate things, adjust the plan, and don't be scared to reprioritise in such scenario. It's critical to include important stakeholders in the process if you want to succeed. At the start of the process, identify who these people are and remind them why the transformation is taking place and what their role is in it.

"Effectively defining roles and duties may result in a 70% boost in transformation success."

Make the modification process as transparent as possible. Not just to key stakeholders, but to everyone in the organisation. It will be less difficult to overcome any resistance to the change. Create a documented communication strategy that covers all issues, including the new organisation's appearance. Ensure that communication is two-way, that it is a discussion, and that workers have the opportunity to ask questions and express their concerns. You could, for example, hold a town hall meeting or even brief 1-on-1 meetings.

It's critical to have complete agreement with all executives on the objective and extent of the change that has to take place. If there is a dispute, put it on the table, work it out, and adjust the plan as required. Just don't wait till the modification is complete. Employees are at the heart of your business. Focus on their requirements throughout the transformation process and keep them updated on the progress. This can also imply removing dysfunctional hierarchies that obstruct development and rearranging teams. Employee-centricity will help you gain employee buy-in and boost the likelihood of success during organisational change and beyond. It will help you figure out how much work you've already completed, how much work you still have ahead of you, and whether or not you need to pivot. Utilise data, get input from workers and consumers, and monitor the success of this long-term transformation. The metrics you use to track your success are determined by your objectives.

If, as in your example, you're trying to update your workplace tools, you may track software uptake as well as improvements in employee experience, performance, and productivity over time. Organisational change, when done correctly, leads to increased performance and a business culture. The process of organisational change, on the other hand, can be lengthy and difficult. That is why, in order to thrive, organisations must break it down into smaller chunks, create goals, and have a clear vision and plan, all while concentrating on their employees.

Assume you want to create the finest organisation to work for on the planet. What would it be like if you could? For the past three years, you've been ideal organisation in surveys and seminars throughout the world. Study on the relationship between authenticity and effective leadership led to this purpose. Simply put, people will not follow a leader who appears to be untrustworthy.

However, the executives we spoke with insisted that in order to be honest, they needed to work for an authentic company. Having strong personal and organisational values, being modest, ethical in all things, treating everyone equally, and remaining collected, calm, and empathic. A visionary sees a future that inspires others, is passionate about it, strategic about it, and is laser-focused on it.

Leaders define their minimal standards of excellence and then go out to demonstrate to others how to achieve them. Teams that collaborate effectively produce amazing results.

Values are key components that guide our decision-making and shape an organisation's culture. Organisational values are a collection of basic ideas or moral concepts that guide people's conduct in organisations. The values of the organisation are those who will help leaders and their teams with decision making and the tradeoffs that occur while we are developing a vision and implementing plans. Urgent action is required to raise awareness, and this process must undoubtedly begin at home, where these principles and values must first be developed and reinforced in a citizen. Organisations also have an essential educational function with regard to their employees, suppliers, and consumers, as well as in informing governments about ethics, justice, and values. All of this will necessitate the formation of "conscious businesses," which are those that have conscious people at all levels of their organisation, shaping the organisational culture to be more balanced, just, and human, and whose vision, values, culture, and processes will generate meaning and value for their stakeholders on a continuous basis.

Strategic planning entails not just thinking about the future, but also acting on it. In the world, we are seeing the emergence of a society in which values are deteriorating. Urgent action is required to boost the degree of consciousness growing, and this process must undoubtedly be strengthened from within. Strategic planning entails not just thinking about the future, but also acting on it.

A major issue with strategic planning that is implemented in organisations is that it should challenge people to think about the future and especially to model it, but it frequently ends up becoming an exclusive tool of analysis of the present, whose activities are usually developed centrally, in a bureaucratic and apathetic manner. Peter Drucker stated that the most likely future "is one in which you believe, shape, and do the required and sufficient steps to construct it." So the destiny of mankind is fundamentally dependent on whatever path we choose to take and how we act to achieve excellence.

Businesses with almost equal possibilities throughout the critical years — bought into the above-mentioned change myths and failed to make the transition from excellent to outstanding. It's a terrible idea to determine where to drive the bus before you've gotten the appropriate people on board and the wrong people off. You won't have to worry about inspiring your passengers if you have the appropriate individuals on board. The appropriate individuals are self-motivated. There's nothing like being part of a team that is expected to provide outstanding outcomes. Nothing else matters if you have the wrong individuals on the bus. Even if you're on the correct track, you won't be able to accomplish greatness. With average employees and a great vision, you'll get mediocre outcomes.

The vision is a strong tool for pushing individuals out of their comfort zones, producing a creative tension that is the energy that comes into action when we define a goal that is at variance with the existing reality, as mentioned in Peter Senge's book The Fifth Discipline. Creativity reminds me of the need to create an atmosphere in which honest mistakes are acknowledged and used as a source of learning, and where differences are respected and cherished, for it is through them that creative thought is developed. On the other hand, seeking consensus means that everyone participating in the process will give in and lose something. On the other hand, valuing all means that everyone involved in the process will give in and lose something. "Unanimity is stupid." Seeking unanimity implies that everyone participating in the process will give in and lose something. On the other hand, valuing all differences and creating something new from them generates purpose and value for everyone involved, and everyone benefits.

When there is a lack of freedom, the human mind becomes more inventive. Expect the constraints to be given to the business environment in the form of indicators or trends; it may be too late to react; the crisis must be created. A vision that shifts the corporate level creates creative tension, which creates a positive crisis.

Consider two people attempting to solve an issue without being aware of this dynamic; the first person's method of thinking is largely black hat, while the second is yellow hat. The person wearing the black hat will argue, "See, how we have this difficulty, that risk, and that point of weakness," whereas the one wearing the yellow hat will disagree, stating, "See, we have this opportunity, we could achieve this benefit, we have these strengths." Who is correct? Who is incorrect? Both are correct and incorrect; the beauty of this strategy is that at a given point in the dynamics, everyone is wearing the same hat, harmonising such circumstances and driving us to think in a different way. Both are correct, but the beauty of this strategy is that at a given point in the dynamics, everyone is wearing the same hat, harmonising such conditions and pushing us to think with a new part of our brain that we are not accustomed to utilising, and this will extract fantastic ideas from the process.

The uncertainties are change factors that connect alternative and opposing universes, diametrically opposed worlds, and this separates them from the megatrend, which is something that will happen sooner or later, to a greater or lesser extent, and has only one direction. Crucial uncertainties are those that have the most influence and unpredictability in the industry or organisation and have the potential to affect the normal flow of operations. They serve as the "raw material" for defining the framework of potential situations. Thus, if two uncertainties are considered crucial to the business, four scenarios are formed by combining two by two of each of the uncertainties' diametrically opposing poles. If three significant uncertainties are specified, eight potential scenarios are constructed.

In practise, dealing with two important uncertainties allows for the development of a solid strategic strategy. More than three key uncertainties in their exploration do not provide cost and value. If it were required to employ the features resulting from more than three significant uncertainties, two or three uncertainties might be combined and transformed into one uncertainty until two or three critical uncertainties are found.

Mapping trends, opportunities, and threats is vital for developing a strategy plan, but the challenge is that they are generally rather powerful signals and hence are clearly detected by all rivals. What competitive benefits might be anticipated from a strategy based on these signals and trends? It must go deeper, and it is critical to pay attention to the faint signals, which are indicators of changes that are likely to occur but are not yet visible. It must also look beyond the organisation's current market to discover what other industries can teach it. It is also critical to identify uncertainties that have the potential to harm or change the foundations of the organisation. And, given this set of uncertainties, determine which of the two or three crucial ones are. However, how does it organise a strategic planning process and the development of corporate strategies in times of increasing frequency and severity of change?

In the current environment, with the globe more connected as a result of the digital revolution, through social networks and mobile connectivity everywhere and at any time, Decentralised and unstructured information is emerging. How do you assemble this collection of data into a strategic plan that makes sense for shaping the future and providing meaning to stakeholders? I have utilised a series of techniques in multi-departmental workshops that have proven effective: competitive intelligence is used to map megatrends. Diagnosis, prioritisation, idea generation, and change management are all hats. To construct prospective scenarios, critical uncertainties must be identified.

Change can be a double-edged sword for businesses, bringing agility and profitability but posing serious difficulties for employees. Therefore, even though change is unpopular and still carries a significant chance of failure, Gartner reports that more than half of change initiatives fail.

Identify opportunities and threats in each prospective scenario, correlate with the strengths and weaknesses identified in the current state diagnosis, and generate strategies and tactics, determining which support is required for each point of attention. Crowdsourcing to map megatrends and provide future vision fragments, addressing specific themes that represent the previously established aim to be reached as previously defined by the business owner.

The information age and the current external market establish a gap between necessity and hesitancy. Understanding the fundamentals of change management enables managers to communicate change to employees in a way that encourages acceptance of transformation by employees members as a beneficial and simple part of their new routine. At the organisational level, change management involves ensuring that change leaders provide managers with the guidance and training they need to give each employee the resources they need to adapt to the changes.

There is no one method that works for all organisations since change management is customised for each one. However, by employing the subsequent change management questions, you can guarantee a successful change project and join the 34% of organisations that successfully implement positive, significant change.

- What effects will the change have on organisation procedures?
- What are the dangers of staying the same?
- Does the change have a strong business case?
- How proficient are they right now?
- What tools and tasks are necessary to get from here to there?
- What IT infrastructure do we have?
- What operational procedures are in place?
- What systems and procedures will we require once the project is finished?
- Is this assessing the attitudes, habits, and culture of the workforce?

- How well will the proposed change be received by the workforce?
- What are the ramifications for the finances?
- How will the modification impact the clients?
- What new abilities will employees require after the transition is complete?
- What positive or negative effects will the change have on the workplace?
- How closely does the existing workplace culture match the one that will be adopted after the project?
- Does the organisational culture need to change for us to be successful?
- What new viewpoints, actions, and attitudes must we instil for the initiative to succeed?
- How do we instil a feeling of urgency in the workforce?
- Employee resistance to change: how often is it and why?
- What is the most effective method for reducing resistance to change?
- How can we transform our idea of the "final state" of the organisation into an engaging narrative for the change?
- Do we have executive sponsors and new leaders in place?
- Have we outlined a comprehensive project strategy?
- Have we created a transparent project roadmap?
- Do we have clear objectives in place?
- Have those aspirations been transformed?
- How can employees be effectively trained to provide them with the abilities necessary to lead change?
- Which obstacles must new leaders eliminate in order to succeed?
- Which modern tools must employees use?
- What is the most effective approach to using those tools?

- What new procedures and systems does the business need to implement?
- What is the most effective method for phasing out outdated methods and implementing fresh ones?
- Planning and project implementation-related queries
- Do we have KPIs and measurements for change management?
- Have new teams been established and given authority to work at each project level?
- Do we have a plan in place to find volunteers?
- Have we developed KPIs and monitoring systems for those metrics?
- Are direct reports being used to acquire data in real-time?
- When will employees members examine metrics?
- How frequently will team leaders get together to assess the success of the project?
- Do we have established accountability?
- Do we have a plan to enhance the performance of change management?
- How frequently will we acknowledge and share our quick victories?
- Do we have a strategy in place for routinely assessing employee feedback?
- Do we have agile procedures in place to get over organisational transformation obstacles?
- How will we be able to tell when the project is finished?
- Have we gathered and prepared the required information and comments about the project's performance?
- What can we infer about the data?
- What lessons should be learned for the next organisational transformation initiatives?

- Is continuing education for employees required?
- Do we have a strategy in place for ongoing training?
- Do we have methods for evaluating the uptake of change?
- Have we put in place ongoing instruments to encourage desired behaviours, such as performance reviews?
- How successful are these techniques for reinforcement?

A narrative description of a future vision told by someone who has travelled to the future and returned to the present to report on what he has seen. Change management entails mapping the drivers of change resistance and developing an action plan to counteract these factors. Determine the level of preparation for the change.

How will you keep leadership at the heart of organisational change management?

It's not a secret. Leaders who are effective generate successful organisations. How? These business executives have a set of good traits that distinguish them from their organisations. We also know that ineffective leaders contribute to dysfunctional corganisations. What are the beneficial qualities of a successful corporate leader? Various business journals investigate and report on these top attributes of successful leaders on a regular basis. The list that emerges is consistent and demonstrates the talents and actions of the most effective leaders. Forbes, Fortune, Inc., and Entrepreneur are among these periodicals. The most often mentioned traits Here are some of the most important characteristics of effective leaders in many sectors and companies of various sizes: In all settings and contexts, integrity means being honest, truthful, trustworthy, consistent, transparent, responsible, and accountable. Speaking, writing, and particularly listening are all ways to create an open two-way information exchange with workers, customers, and others. Positive, brave, fearless, and optimistic, with a preference for decisive action and outcomes.

A vision that does not stem from a plan is only a fantasy. To make it a reality, it is necessary to coordinate the vision's construction through a project roadmap and oversee each project's implementation. Every project must have the following components: scope, responsibility, a to-do list with a beginning, middle, and end, as well as the right allocation of resources. It is also critical to create a management ritual to monitor the evolution and possible course corrections. Megatrends are events that drastically alter the way people think, manage, purchase, create, socialise, communicate, and so on. Before the workshop sessions, they should be mapped using competitive intelligence tools. You may use them to identify opportunities and risks that need to be addressed. SWOT analysis is a strategic planning technique that is widely used in the corporate sector.

However, all organisations are looking at the same megatrends, with the exception of companies that have a great idea of differentiation. There is a high probability that companies have been looking for the same opportunities and threats and, at the end of the day, are going to compete for the same things in a "Red Ocean." The "Six Hats" method is used to construct a diagnostic by gathering the strengths and weaknesses of the current state using the first three hats: The colour white is associated with facts and data collection. Black is associated with issue identification, dangers, critical judgement, and the flaws of the organisation. The goal of this hat is to collect information on the organisation's strengths and key capabilities. The Blue Hat is constantly used for prioritising and project planning; the Green Hat is used to create the vision as well as the generation of ideas for strategic projects; and finally, the Red Hat is used to map the issues of change management: mitigating the detractors' effects and enhancing the facilitators for project roadmap implementation. The "Six Hats" approach developed by Edward de Bono is a group discussion methodology employing colourful hats that establish a natural discipline, including parallel thinking related to the concepts, helping the group to think together more effectively.

Leaders build trust and develop teams by assisting each member in working in a transparent and accountable manner. Any successful business should be built on the foundation of honesty and sincerity. Two creatures are shown in this drawing: a fox and a hedgehog. Which of the two are you? According to an old Greek tale, hedgehogs know one large thing, but foxes know many minor things. It turns out that all good-to-great leaders are hedgehogs. They understand how to reduce a complicated world to a single organising principle—the type of fundamental concept that unites, organizes, and leads all decisions. That isn't to argue that hedgehogs are simple creatures. Leaders of good-to-great firms build hedgehogs. A concept that is basic yet represents piercing insight and deep understanding, similar to great thinkers who take complexity and reduce it down into simple, yet profound, concepts (Adam Smith and the invisible hand, Darwin and evolution).

There are two general types of leaders: formal and informal. Under the pretext of a specific rank or position, a leader who has been designated as such and has been granted certain authorities to carry out the duty. A formal leader is not a natural leader since they are chosen or elected in a bureaucratic organisation through a procedure for a specific period of time, with specific powers delegated to the extent that organisational goals and objectives are met. Leaders are the heroes and assets of the organisations or communities to which they belong, and they have the basic goal of completing the task set before them with the help of their groups with confidence. It is one of the leader's duties and responsibilities to properly communicate the task to the group and muster up their courage in all the ways required, to take suggestions from the group members to evaluate the group members' attitude, and to coordinate the efforts of the group members.

The leadership and the rest of the organisation disagree on fundamental issues. Employees are not as enthusiastic about new corporate initiatives as they once were.The workplace has become toxic; morale is low, new hires feel isolated, employees are unconcerned about results, and your best employees have gone silent. Yes, it's time to make a shift. But what precisely is it? What do you do first? Business strategy is influenced by cultural factors. Deloitte's global culture model identifies eight categories in which executives must make deliberate choices and judgments in order to realign culture with business objectives. There are several specific places where disruption must occur in order for organisational culture to change course in the middle of the game.

"The pessimist complains about the wind. The optimist expects it to change. The leader adjusts the sails."
-John Maxwell

A leader must possess the following abilities in order to achieve organisational goals and objectives and increase his group's efficiency. Leadership is the ability of an organisation to build strength in the form of manpower confidence and high morale, both of which lead to the organisation's profitability. This is only achievable when the organisation's leaders or leadership stay educated about the demands of the organisation.

A task is a test of an organisation's capacity to function in any environment, such as a critical and tough period, by making the best and most beneficial decisions possible. Coordination between leadership and manpower is a critical component for an organisation's success and completion of difficult tasks. Too many leaders have no idea what they don't know and have no desire to learn. Blind spots, on the other hand, can emerge in predictable ways and can be addressed. Much like driving a car, you can't be effective if there are vast, dangerous blind zones all around you. Approximately half of the employees promoted to C-level leadership roles inside a organisation perform below expectations. Your cross-functional team will emerge from leadership for organisational excellence cohesive, collaborative, and focused on a single goal. They'll make organisational breakthroughs in strategy, procedure, and execution.

"Great leaders are ordinary individuals who possess specific characteristics that distinguish them from others and enable them to accomplish amazing results."

Regardless of cultural, gender, or age disparities, all leaders who have been true inspirations to their teams exhibit similar patterns of behavior. Staying self-aware, courteous of others, intuitive, instinctive, anticipatory, and aware of the work environment are all examples of mindfulness. Initiator: inventing new streams of people, goods, services, processes, markets, and activities to ensure the organisation's long-term prosperity. Supportive behavior includes being trustworthy, establishing trust, delegating, being responsive, focused, and engaged, as well as cooperating and collaborating. Being principled means having strong personal and organisational values, being modest, and acting ethically in all situations.

As a result of the uncertainty, an us-versus-them mindset emerges, causing even more division and mistrust. Increased division leads to a decline in empathy and self-awareness. It becomes practically hard to perceive the situation from the other person's point of view, as well as to be self-aware and modest enough to confess errors. When acts are viewed through this lens of mistrust and secrecy, they are more likely to be taken negatively, resulting in drama. The us-versus-them mentality becomes permissive, and bad behavior is tolerated. And tolerance invariably breeds more heinous actions since the bad actor is emboldened by the tolerance.

After all, in our society, problems are always attributed to the person on the other side. As a result, you fail to see circumstances objectively and instead see them through the prism of expedient blame. You cloak yourselves under the guise of "business choices." The absence of transparency is a classic example. Organisations construct shrouds of secrecy because they believe they are forbidden from discussing "confidential," "private," or "personal" information. In certain cases, the information on why someone was reprimanded or penalised is inaccurate or incomplete.

In others, it's implementing large-scale corporate changes (reorganisations, leadership changes, and so on) behind an impenetrable wall, with no employee involvement or knowledge. Regardless of the specific secret, two lessons stand out: Employees know more than you believe they do trying to deceive them is clear to them, and you end up doing more harm than good since they realise you're lying employees. It truly does pay to be honest, as old-fashioned as it may sound. Confusing unjust and unlawful behavior, an unequal playing field (or the reasonable sense of one), and secrecy do not go together nicely. This sends one of two messages to employees. The first is this: don't come to me with a complaint unless it's about illegal behavior. Employers don't find out about difficulties until they've reached a crisis point when this happens. The second lesson is that when you do raise your issues, use charged legal rhetoric like "hostile work environment" and "retaliation" instead of stating facts and consequences.

As a result, rather than solving problems, the organisation leader goes into defense mode. This merry-go-round of posturing demonstrates the need to establish a shared and effective business vocabulary—one that genuinely aims to solve the workplace drama problem. As one side believes the other is out to get them, blind spots form, and our capacity to predict and respond to drama deteriorates. Of course, shifting someone to a lesser position on the organisational chart during a reorganisation may cause resentment and accusations of injustice, but reorganisation strategists believe, "Hey, they're lucky to have a job."

The capacity to foresee and plan for dramais a crucial talent that, sadly, most businesses lack. Clearly, the solution is to start recruiting everyone who ticks the "diversity box" regardless of qualifications. While this may address your short-term financial problem, it will surely build animosity, harm your business, and do little to assist with "diversity statistics" in the long run because you are putting the prospects up to fail. You execute ineffective solutions or overcorrect because we don't recognise the fundamental reasons for the drama. In either scenario, we exacerbate an already difficult situation. In today's workplace, the most common response to workplace drama is to "examine your policies and procedures." There are more rules. HR and leadership are increasingly seen as police, exacerbating the drama rather than alleviating it.

Leaders may influence their workplace to reflect ethical behavior as a key value by providing an example. They lay down guidelines for people to follow as well as goals that they should strive for. Inspirational leaders are enthused by the prospect of the future and encourage their teams to share their vision of what the organisation may become.

The best leaders, in particular, are excellent team builders. They interact and connect with others, are natural networkers, are active in recognising and rewarding great work, are persuasive, and have a strong understanding of their objectives. Legacy leaders, above all, are genuine. Authenticity attracts and motivates those who share your values. When we think, say, and act from our heart and soul—our actual inner self—we are being authentic. Being real in business takes guts because we become vulnerable when we allow our often-protected inner self to be seen.

The benefits of established soul-to-soul and heart-to-heart ties, on the other hand, can be substantial. Southwest Airlines' Herb Keller, Amazon's Jeff Bezos, Starbucks' Howard Schultz, Apple's Steve Jobs (and his successor Tim Cook), and Walmart's Sam Walton are just a few examples of brilliant leaders who embodied these talents. Henry Ford, Thomas Edison, and George Eastman (Kodak), according to history, were excellent commercial executives.

And there are plenty more.

What does it take for your organisation to come up with a hedgehog concept? Begin by addressing the harsh realities. During the transition from excellent to outstanding, the management atmosphere resembles a raging scientific discussion, with clever, tough-minded individuals scrutinising hard data and disputing what those findings imply. The goal isn't to win the discussion, but to come up with the greatest solutions and, in the end, to settle on a viable hedgehog concept. Kimberly-Clark emerged as the world's leading paper-based consumer-products organisation, topping P&G in six of eight categories and outright controlling its longtime archrival, Scott Paper. Kimberly-Clark outperformed the market by four times under Darwin Smith, comfortably outperforming such renowned organisations as Coca-Cola, General Electric, Hewlett-Packard, and 3M. Take a peek at your workstation. If you're like most hard-charging bosses, you have a well-articulated to-do list.

We've all heard that leaders are the ones who make things happen, and it's true: it takes a lot of work to push that flywheel. But it's also true that good-to-great leaders stand out for their unwavering determination to quit doing anything that doesn't fit neatly into their Hedgehog Concept. Darwin Smith and his management team faced a challenge when developing the Hedgehog Concept for Kimberly-Clark. On the one hand, they saw that the greatest way to greatness was through the consumer industry, where the corporation had established world-class capacity in the development of the Kleenex brand.

Overcorrection is just as harmful as applying the incorrect solution. This, too, stems from a failure to consider what may truly fix the problem, critically and creatively. Your organisation's diversity indicators reflect a low number of underrepresented employees. Clearly, the solution is to start recruiting everyone who ticks the "diversity box" regardless of their qualifications.

"I think the combination of graduate education in a field like Computer Science and the opportunity to apply this in a work environment like Microsoft is what drove me. The impact these opportunities create can lead to work that has a broad, worldwide impact" – Satya Nadella

Leaders open up tremendous opportunities for everyone if they work together as a team. Great leaders question the status quo and search for methods to achieve the same thing in a more efficient manner. They are willing to try new things, are not afraid of taking risks, and see failures as opportunities to learn. Jim Collins and his colleagues were led to crucial themes by a number of unanticipated discrepancies when evaluating and coding the many aspects of the good-to-great organisations and their comparisons. Bringing in high-profile, celebrity CEOs to whip a organisation into shape actually hurts a organisation's capacity to go from excellent to outstanding. "Strategy," defined as the creation of a long-term plan of any type, has no link to good-to-great performance. Long-term plans were in place for both the good-to-great and comparative organisations. When it came to making the move from excellent to outstanding, technology was unimportant. It aids in the acceleration of a transition, but it is not essential for it to begin.

In my experience, successful people shoot for the stars, put their hearts on the line in every battle, and ultimately discover that the lessons learned from the pursuit of excellence mean much more than the immediate trophies and glory. - Josh Waitzkin

A good leader is aware of each of his team members' talents and flaws. He may free up time to focus on higher-level activities by distributing jobs correctly and trusting the team with his ideas. Recognising individual contributions and celebrating triumphs works wonders, and leaders that do so motivate their employees to work twice as hard! Genuine gratitude fuels perseverance and encourages teams to work with authenticity. A lack of authenticity leads to inconsistency, which is typically manifested as a failure to apply solutions evenly.

"The single biggest way to impact an organisation is to focus on leadership development. There is almost no limit to the potential of an organisation that recruits good people, raises them up as leaders and continually develops them." -John Maxwell

Over time, this leads to genuine inequity and also creates a strong perception of a lack of workplace justice. Is it unfair or illegal? Repeated inconsistency in dealing with conflict (e.g., ignoring misconduct, conducting sham investigations into claims of misconduct, uneven distribution of consequences when misconduct is proven) not only erodes trust, but also increases the likelihood that any level of misconduct will be perceived as not only unfair, but also illegal. This raises the likelihood that they may file internal or external legal claims. If the mistake is made internally, the employer must follow the rules and undertake a formal workplace inquiry. Alternatively, the employee might file a lawsuit. There is also another option in today's social media–fueled environment. A grievance filed by an employee might end up on a blog, an employer review website, a social networking site, or as a front-page exposé in a major newspaper. An employment lawsuit could have been yesterday's top workplace dread. Today, brand value may be destroyed with the single click of a button. A button that says "publish."

Every organisation starts with a vision, a concept that drives the organisation forward. This finally spreads out and gives an organisation an appropriate structure. It's the equivalent of starting a family. Some people fail, while others live happily ever after. You won't be able to achieve the results you want until you have an employee-centric culture that prioritises their well-being. The bottom line is that you want to keep your employees happy and give them positive experiences.

Your employees apply your leadership principles to guide their work, which defines your work culture. Strive to be Earth's Best Employer is one of them. It is a value that urges leaders to lead with empathy, enjoy themselves at work, and make it simple for others to enjoy themselves. The other is that success and scale bring with them a great deal of responsibility. This album challenges leaders to be modest and careful about the consequences of their actions (especially the unintended consequences), as well as to be accountable to their local communities, the environment, and future generations.

For many people in corporate world , the idea of apologising is unthinkable. It is, nevertheless, a necessary component if you are to shift the needle on culture. You all make errors. You are incapable of anticipating issues. You don't give ourselves enough time to make sound judgments. You disregard issues in the hope that they will go away. Making a mistake is human; neglecting to acknowledge and rectify the situation is catastrophic. Inauthentic companies are made up of CEOs that refuse to confess wrongdoing, prolonging the cycle of mistrust. These triggers, if left unchecked, produce a poor work atmosphere and have concrete (and negative) consequences. Widespread distrust results in low morale and productivity, as well as significant (and unneeded) turnover, increasing allegations of injustice, difficulty recruiting and maintaining top people, legal claims, and, of course, brand harm.

Leaders must clearly define the goal and integrate it into all organisation efforts. On its part, "People Practises" must accept it comprehensively in text and spirit. The business and operational procedures must keep up with the pace. Every stage of the trip requires infrastructure and systems to support it. And, at any given time, all thinking and activity must be mapped forward to the overarching goal of the organisational journey. In the video below, Deloitte uses a five-lever method to maximise cultural re-engineering.

A leader is someone who uses threats or authority to exert influence on subordinates and others solely for the good or welfare of the community or groups that chose or elected him/her as their leader. It is not useless to state that a leader is someone who motivates others and encourages them to obey him or her willingly rather than under duress. A leader is a person who represents his community's or group's desires and needs and whose activities are solely for the welfare and benefit of that group.

To sum up, leadership plays a critical role in the advancement of companies. Only co-ordination and confidence across concerns and groups of concerns can produce effective and meaningful work, and only the function of leadership can achieve this co-ordination and confidence, since business concerns cannot meet the needs of every single employee or member of the workforce. As a result, by working together, the organisation can achieve its goals and the groups may achieve their own goals that are aligned with the organisation's.

Organisational success requires both management and leadership. When an organisation has great administration but no leadership, the result can be suffocating and bureaucratic. In contrast, if an organisation lacks management, the result might be meaningless or misdirected change for the sake of change. Organisations must nurture both competent management and skillful leadership in order to be successful. Organisations perform best when internal and external communication channels are flawless.

As a result, effective businesses handle data on a constant basis. Information management is the science of processing information to assist managers in making informed decisions. However, the routes through which this information is transmitted should be secured to preserve the security of the organisation's private information, which may otherwise be exposed to unwanted third-party intrusion.

It is advised that both employers and workers understand that in order to create an organisational environment where all people are happier, if an employee feels confident in his or her career prospects, he or she will feel more at ease in his or her workplace.

As a result, if you want to know why there are such divisions inside the organisation, you need look into all of the aforementioned reasons or causes for such discontent. You may also begin doing all of the measures outlined above to you're your organisation a fantastic place to work.

There should be systems in place to maintain employees in a healthy and stable state of mind while doing their duties of serving the organisation's interests through regulated ethical communication models. Expected behaviour, procedural patterns, and responses to deviations are all defined by these models. The idea underpinning risk estimating and evaluation is that logical inferences may be drawn about the chance of a risk occurring and its possible repercussions.

Setting a goal and then devising a strategy to attain it is a typical practise in any organisation. All organisations obey the rules, but only a few are able to meet or surpass their goals. The disparity in results is attributable to the organisation's strategy. Organisations that can effectively and efficiently execute and manage their resources stand out from the crowd. Motivation, empowerment, and training are the key positive influences on successful organisational behaviour.

In order to create a proactive mindset among employees, these elements should be incorporated into a organisation. Incentives, promotions, awards, and recognition are just a few of the motivation-boosting techniques. The planning component is critical in de-mystifying poor performance as a result of employee redundancy. Because the degree of success is dependent on social interaction abilities, the appropriate implementation of a competence evaluation system is directly proportionate to employee performance.

An emotion testing programme is implemented to assess employees' emotional attitudes toward one another, followed by a counselling session to ensure that employees are concerned about their coworkers' social needs. Because difficulties that each individual experiences on an interpersonal level eventually influence the group, it is critical to build a healthy work environment and personal growth views that apply to all situations in order to enhance productive behaviour.

Organisational psychologists should conduct in-depth investigations into each employee's personal life in order to identify which behavioural treatment best matches the individual. A good working environment should be flexible, relevant, and pleasant, all while adhering to measurement criteria that support the intrinsic and extrinsic effects that the environment has on employee performance.

Leadership would be powerless without leadership's efforts asthe backbone of ideas, and leadership would be worthless if it did not provide a systems-based management framework. Leaders that are ethically sound and willing to sacrifice conveniences for aims and objectives strive for innovation and societal betterment. Leadership and management, like the iceberg and the disciplines, are both autonomous and reliant on one another, especially when attaining goals in a learning organisation.

There should be tailored to a unique work environment, employee talents, and organisational objectives. Furthermore, the size of an organisation and the nature of its responsibilities must be considered. Within each business, numerous elements such as incentives, advancement, and a structured feedback system impact organisational behaviour. Policies geared towards balancing performance and conduct, on the other hand, should be connected with an organisation's goals in order to be effective.

Every leader has a distinct perspective about what makes a organisation culture successful. However, healthy workplaces share certain similarities, such as worker autonomy, open communication, clear direction, genuine relationships, and aligned values. Creating, scaling, and maintaining an authentic organisation culture is an ongoing and intentional process. As the business landscape and global climate changes, corporate culture needs to grow to fit worker needs and desires. Reading organisational culture books helps professionals gain the skills and mindsets necessary to make their companies great places to work. The effort to support employees ultimately pays off, as companies with great work cultures see reduced turnover, inspire more brand loyalty, and are better equipped to weather inevitable adversity.

As a result, as a cure for inclusion and active involvement, which translates into ideal performance, it is vital to balance feedback with the aims of such an organisation. In general, risk is seen as a negative aspect in the implementation of new technology in an organisation because of the potential for unrealised advantages, technical performance deficiencies, schedule slippage, cost overruns, and worker disengagement. It's critical to have a robust plan in place to handle the risks that come with adopting new concepts like technological efficiency.

In practise, dealing with two important uncertainties allows for the development of a solid strategic strategy. More than three key uncertainties in their exploration do not provide cost and value. If it were required to employ the features resulting from more than three significant uncertainties, two or three uncertainties might be combined and transformed into one uncertainty until two or three critical uncertainties are found.

The SWOT approach was used in each of the situations that were generated. The big difference here is that because the uncertainties that have been set are critical for business and, depending on the direction that it will follow, could change the business strategy profoundly, with this methodology, it doesn't matter what this trend is, because the organisation has prepared for it all prospective scenarios generated by the combination of uncertainties. Crowdsourcing is the act of gathering ideas and collecting contributions from a diverse set of individuals via an online community in order to produce solutions to a particular problem. Storytelling is the capacity to convey relevant stories, in this case about a future vision. This approach, as well as all of the data gathered from the other tools, is then used to construct a picture of the future, describing each point of the aim stated by the business owner.

This temporal dimension has psychological significance because it is not a very small amount of time in which individuals will not offer anything out of the ordinary. This time dimension has psychological significance because if it is not a very short period of time, people will not propose anything out of the box, because change would not be feasible in this period of time, and if it is too far, the proposals will have little meaning, because people will not be present to see this reality materialise.

Furthermore, the process dynamics have the capacity to engage individuals and, more importantly, keep the organisation compromised with the strategic plan's implementation. This effect is caused by the following factors: because the teams were involved in the description of the vision through the concept of crowdsourcing, they felt like co-owners of the story, which has a power multiplier by the ease of communication and also because it stirs the collective consciousness of the organisation.

As with the industrial revolution and the internet, we are on the verge of a new breakthrough. The smart object age will usher in the new era. New enterprises will arise from this tipping point, and the traits that organisations must apply in their culture in order to surf this new period must be nimble. New organisations will emerge from this tipping point, and the features of these organisations that want to ride this new period must include nimble methods to reinvent and evolve their business, goods, and services while striving for perfection in customer experience. This operational style is more akin to startups, which includes characteristics such as speed, flexibility, and a willingness to take calculated risks in order to capitalise on possibilities that appear on the horizon. This trait is best articulated by the effectuation idea, which suggests a mix of learning by doing and trial and error, built on four pillars: acceptable losses, strategic partnerships, exploitation, and an uncertain future.

Large organisations will find it difficult to navigate this terrain because their success has been built on developing processes and procedures that are structured to ensure repeatability, but those who can create an environment with isolated spaces where internal startups can be protected temporarily from old paradigms and structured processes until they can be generated will have both united agility in capturing new business and the ability to perpetuate it.

Managers that follow the conventional approach think that the best approach to achieving excellence is to create a set of systems, policies, procedures, and regulations that control every decision made in the organisation. It takes years to build and define these. The ultimate objective is to safeguard everyone in the organisation against their own shortcomings. This swiftly devolves into safeguarding the organisation from individual shortcomings. There are additional regulations governing which decisions managers may and cannot make. To cover every eventuality, several layers of management must be established, resulting in a cumbersome organisational structure in which decisions are continually pushed "up the ladder." This motivates managers to use passive-defensive leadership strategies, which leads to the formation of a passive-defensive culture. There are passive-defensive cultures in which everyone is urged to comply, push choices up the chain of command, and resist change. People advance by being pleasant, according to the rules, and avoiding accountability.

Although the initial purpose was to strive for greatness, this gradually morphed into one of sustaining the status quo. Employees are disengaged in organisations with a passive-defensive culture, as evidenced by high turnover and or excessive sick pay. The service and product quality are always subpar at best and sometimes sub-par. An aggressive approach is adopted by managers who, like the preceding managers, have a basic belief that people would not perform effectively if left to their own devices. They, on the other hand, believe in deeds rather than words. Managers here utilise an aggressive-defensive style, requiring employees to work long, hard hours and never make a mistake. They micromanage with an autocratic style that is always looking for defects and blunders.

This strategy produces an aggressive-defensive culture in which mistakes are not tolerated, individuals compete with one another rather than collaborate, and everyone is driven to work long, hard hours. This method can produce short-term results. In the long run, however, service and product quality are irregular at best. Employee turnover and burnout are high. Simply recruit tyrants as managers and hold everyone responsible for learning on their own and generating outcomes, no matter the cost. As previously said, in the quest for perfection, this method might offer short-term results. When the benefits end, the business implements additional aggressive-defensive strategies aimed at achieving results at the cost of their most important resource—their people.

The objective of these new measurements shifts from the pursuit of excellence to the pursuit of perfection—where "heads roll" at the tiniest of errors. Individuals in this culture ignore the notion of continuous progress, focus on insignificant details, and push people into a 24/7 dedication to the cause.

Even calculated risks and thinking "beyond the box" are abandoned as people try to escape penalties. People advance in their careers by working long hours, never making a mistake, and having the capacity to dominate and influence others. A constructive approach necessitates that the business and its management team recognise that the pursuit of excellence can only be attained when leaders believe in their people and invest time and effort in developing them. They understand that everyone wants to perform well and will strive for perfection if given the chance and resources to do so.

As a result, there is a constructive culture in which individual effort is valued, employees are encouraged to take measured risks, and people are held accountable for service or product quality. People are also encouraged to participate in decision-making by offering unique and creative ideas. They are required to treat one another with decency and respect, as well as collaborate and assist others. The end product is nothing short of spectacular.

Employees in constructive environments are often engaged, with minimal turnover and sick pay (people are literally healthier in these cultures). They also cite not only excellent levels of service and product quality, but also a culture of continuous improvement. These companies are achieving goals that were thought "pie-in-the-sky" and unattainable just a few years ago. The Pursuit of Excellence is expanded to include a persistent pursuit of excellence.

Which approach and culture are you looking for?

The conventional approach is time-consuming, but it is secure. People know what to expect on a daily basis. They are disengaged yet determined to maintain the status quo and avoid "rocking the boat." Staying out of trouble takes a "back seat" to service and product excellence.

The aggressive approach is simple to adopt. Leaders do not require training or growth; they only need the power and skill to keep others responsible. This strategy can yield short-term benefits, but it frequently comes at the price of the individuals doing the work. It is typical to have high levels of burnout and turnover. Organisations, on the other hand, can adopt measures to compensate for predicted turnover if people are not a valued resource. On the plus side, if the senior management team is hands-on, competent, and prepared to work long, hard hours, this sort of culture may be maintained with infrequent success. They must also be prepared to accept greater stress and the associated stress-related sickness. All of this can be frightening for managers, especially if they feel employees should be handled like children, micromanaged, disciplined, and subjected to a slew of regulations. However, the outcomes of a constructive culture vastly surpass those of other civilizations. The employees are enthusiastic, and everyone strives to give excellent service and product quality. In other words, it ensures the organisation's long-term existence and growth.

How businesses may cope with human fallibility in order to foster workplace excellence?

Some workplace blunders endanger lives, while others pave the way for inventive innovations. An organisation requires a communication atmosphere where it is acceptable to express viewpoints, confess mistakes, and seek for support in crucial situations in order to cope constructively with fallibility.

This chapter focuses on emotional intelligence, which has been identified as a factor in excellent on-the-job performance and the capacity to live a successful life. The chapter deviates from typical methodologies by emphasizing on non-cognitive rather than cognitive skills to explain and predict performance and achievements. It is based on a rising country, India. It finds that those with strong intrinsic non-cognitive skills such as trustworthiness, conscientiousness, adaptability, initiative, and commitment have a better chance of becoming effective leaders with enhanced service-orientation, empathy, and conflict management skills—all of which are desirable traits in any organisation striving for efficiency.

It also indicates that, while such intangible, internal talents are important, they cannot replace obvious psycho-social characteristics and that, as a result, effective recruiting tactics must include behavioural as well as cognitive skills.

The world has changed. The previous method of managing (but not resolving) employee conflict is no longer effective. Every organisation's openness has risen as a result of social media, and our shifting demographics make it more crucial than ever to be genuine and foster a healthy working culture. The # MeToo movement is the result of employers' resolving conflicts in the wrong way. That doesn't imply, as you'll see in " Redefining Organisational Excellence", taking steps that might put you at risk of claims. It entails broadening your perspective and treating the workplace as a whole, rather than just focusing on the symptoms (claims) of a toxic workplace culture. You'll learn about the core causes of workplace critical situation, as well as what is most likely to lead to sexual harassment at work, which is very pertinent in today's context. Given that we are in the midst of a cultural shift over what constitutes suitable and incorrect workplace behavior, the themes discussed in this book are a must-read for any organisation leader, rising leader, or employee who wants to understand how to avoid any workplace critical situation.

"When everything seems to be going against you, remember that the airplane takes off against the wind, not with it." - Henry Ford

The capacity of an organisation to function efficiently, adapt properly, adjust correctly, and grow from within is referred to as organisational health. People, processes, structures, systems, behaviours, and governance are all characteristics of a good organisation. It's one in which suitable adaptation, maintenance, and development actions are critical to preserving operational performance and alignment. Organisational health examines the key and interrelated parts of an organisation that must be kept in good working order for managers to achieve their objectives. Understanding and assessing organisational health; the impact of structures on organisational health, such as hierarchies, alliances, and joint ventures; maintenance and development, including organisational development, change management, learning, and workplace environment; sustainability, including carbon footprint and business ecosystems; and indicators of health and dysfunction are all covered using a practical, structured approach.

Prepare for limited performance and poor outcomes if you're locked in an old leadership paradigm. With the pace of change increasing by the day, it's more critical than ever to cultivate a positive and enabling culture. In this chapter on organisational excellence, you will learn how to excite and engage people, fix problems that will have an immediate impact on your bottom line, and assist employees in overcoming their toughest hurdles to outperform your competitors.

I look at whether great leaders are born or made, how lean ideas are used differently in various organisations, and why clever individuals fail so often after being promoted to management positions. Take a path that leads to significant performance increases and a great culture where everyone is prepared to succeed with this leadership.

It's difficult to comprehend the extent to which creativity has influenced your life. Imagine being able to snap your fingers and make all the results of human creativity—everything man-made—disappear. What would happen if your world changed? The creative process results in reality. Reality is constructed by humans. Understanding how the creative process becomes stifled and understanding how to release its force and energy turns creativity into execution excellence. Excellence refers to how well a strategy is carried out.

I would offer the most effective tactics and step-by-step instructions for you to construct your own organisational road to excellence. You'll learn how to concentrate on achieving greatness while living and enjoying life to the fullest. You'll develop a more optimistic attitude, more concentrated dedication, better ways to deal with distractions and demands, and tactics for conquering challenges. You'll also find better methods to collaborate with colleagues, respond more effectively to coaching and mentoring, and become more positive and self-directed in your thoughts and actions, resulting in more personal and professional pleasure.

This book attempts to provide insights into the many pathways, courses, and drives that world-class enterprises have constructed in order to achieve the pinnacles of greatness. It also includes an empirical analysis of leadership, a simple and practical conceptual model of what leadership is, and an actionable guide for developing competitive spirit, achieving sustained performance, achieving durable influencing capacity, assisting others in bringing change, and assisting in the actualization of human potential in all roles and levels. It contains the ideas, views, experiences, beliefs, viewpoints, and forward-thinking thoughts of some of the best management and business minds in the world.

These "quick fix" organisational leaders frequently pursue the newest trend, go from one thing to the next, are narrowly focused on a small number of results, are unwilling to reconsider their management strategies, are activity-oriented, and have not achieved substantial internal alignment.

A long-term perspective, a results-driven approach that considers all aspects of organisational performance, process-based approaches, strategic thinking, perseverance and discipline, the ability to improve, and the constant need for alignment (of people, processes, plans, and results) are just a few of the requirements for organisational excellence. It is impossible to achieve organisational excellence "by next year." However, it is a worthy endeavour for businesses that want to develop a real competitive edge that will benefit their clients and communities for many years.

Although there is no one way to lead an organisation toward organisational excellence (since it relies on its vision, particular goals, and starting place), there is, luckily, a definition that is almost universal. The Criteria have been characterised as an "integrated management framework," in the simplest words possible—a tool for comprehending and controlling organisational performance. They are a series of inquiries that serve as a framework for managing any business, regardless of its size or industry.

"Leadership is lifting a person's vision to high sights, the raising of a person's performance to a higher standard, the building of a personality beyond its normal limitations."
-Peter Drucker

People in every business devise new techniques to escape the unpleasantness of change. Diverting attention away from the problem (e.g., denying the problem exists, focusing on only the technical aspects, creating a surrogate conflict, refusing to consider certain options, using humour to lower the temperature, forming new committees) and displacing responsibility (e.g., blaming/scapegoating others both inside and outside the organisation, marginalising those who have raised the issue) are two of the most common work avoidance strategies.

An agile organisation can swiftly adjust to an ever-changing reality. I used to refer to the world as "VUCCAD," which stands for "volatile, uncertain, complex, critical, ambiguous, and dynamic" but now it's a "VUCCAD" world on steroids. Change is happening at a breakneck speed.

Research shows that organisations with strong cultures that encourage adaptation do better financially than those that don't. In this book, I've explored five measures that leaders can take to become more flexible, including stressing both well-being and purpose, cultivating an adaptive mindset, deepening human relationships, and creating a safe learning environment.

Organisational silos, unclear strategy, and delayed decision-making, according to the CEOs, regularly obstruct initiatives to increase work productivity. Building speedier decision-making systems, boosting internal communication and cooperation, and increasing the number of employees are the three main ways that leaders perceive to solve these obstacles. Executives are supervising a seismic shift in how organisations function as a result of the pandemic, ranging from tactical changes in areas like meeting format and cadence, and day-to-day management, to enterprise-wide changes in leadership and people management, technology use, and innovation.

For most CEOs, creating a future-ready organisation will be a tremendous task. Nobody can accurately forecast the future, nor does anybody have a clear vision of it. Short-term skills and long-term strategic aim must be balanced culturally. In practise, the present serves as a vital source of funding for the future. It is crucial to focus on developing an organisational culture that enables organisations to adapt, crystallise, and execute on plan as the future becomes increasingly obvious before attempting to design long-term strategies for the future.

"Organisations will need to constantly adapt and create an organisational culture that encourages ongoing learning and growth. Success will depend on innovation."

Today, no sector or company is immune to disruption, yet many companies are ill-equipped to adapt rapidly enough to withstand the consequences of rapid change. In the second year of the pandemic, the workplace became a fraught battleground, with employees seeing opportunities to rethink what they wanted out of work and participating in the so-called "great resignation" and employers attempting to define a new normal while COVID-19 and its variants wreaked havoc on even the best-laid plans.

You looked for organisations that were either providing the kinds of tools that were designed to create a thriving, positive environment regardless of whether work was done in person, hybrid, or fully remote, or that inherently understood the nature of this tumult and adapted their policies and approaches to serve employees in this charged environment. You are continuously on the lookout for new trends to keep up with. Leaders and entrepreneurs should, however, avoid becoming overawed by the future or the upheaval that is, in large part, being brought about by technology. They have to contribute to co-creating the future.

"Technology won't determine the course of history. Geographics shouldn't determine the future. We are here to create our future. We have the ability to create the future we choose."

Organisations do not adapt quickly enough to keep up with changing requirements, and governance and management methods do not generate the required results. Ineffective communication exacerbates these issues. The development of a good Organisation Performance System(OPS) can help to solve these issues. The contents of this book will provide a deep reservoir of ideas and techniques for producing remarkable outcomes, competitive advantage, and long-term results for leaders, consultants, and organisation advisors.

To summarise, the roles of leadership and management can function in various ways while still being the same when it comes to the development of a organisation. Effective techniques for managing businesses into the future include developing and methodically arranging recruiting philosophies, institutional regulations, budgeting procedures, incentives, and decision-making approaches.

To conclude this chapter, it is critical to recognise that whichever leadership or management style is adopted, it must be related to underlying principles. In essence, the iceberg under the surface is not formed in a single day; it is moulded and nourished throughout the course of one's life by natural and social events, assumptions, and fundamental beliefs. It's vital for leaders to recognise their own icebergs and consider how their beliefs influence their leadership styles and management techniques. In order to be successful in a future society, prospective leaders and managers must first define and develop their own particular leadership style.

"Organisational excellence encompasses the whole spectrum of corporate management and the way the entire business is conducted, with the goal of achieving world-class status."
-Dr. Amit Das

CHAPTER TWO

Impact of Talent Management on Achieving Organisational Excellence

"Organisational energy is a strong and tried-and-true strategy for transforming businesses. Its strength arises from a new view of organisations as living systems with their own vital energy, rather than as mechanical machines chasing financial goals."

Following COVID-19, a huge number of employees left their present employers in search of higher pay, more recognition, more flexible scheduling, and other perks. This phenomenon, known as the "great resignation," had an influence on numerous businesses throughout the world. The past two years have been the most challenging for India Inc., and they have taught us a lot about our identities as societies, as people, and as guardians of the weakest among us. It was a morality test to see what type of society we wanted to create after the epidemic. Transformation became a priority for many companies as a result of the irrevocable changes that the globe underwent. It is more difficult than ever for organisations to choose the best employees, support the digital transition, and enhance the employee experience. Empathy has made a comeback in the managerial vocabulary.

This phenomenon, known as the "great resignation," had an influence on numerous businesses throughout the world. According to the U.S. Bureau of Labor Statistics, a total of 4 million Americans will have left their employment by July 2021, a far greater rate of employee resignations than in the majority of economies. How can recruiting managers keep employees after this resignation tsunami? Understanding people better is the first step in addressing the underlying causes of these startling figures. Data-driven strategies must be used to improve retention. In order to enable human resource professionals and leaders to make better decisions and develop skilled employees, smarter talent management systems that are science-based and real-time are urgently required. Every employee's daily life is impacted by the interactions and business practises of their talent managers. Similar to this, HR practises that support employees' growth and success contribute to the development of a committed and knowledgeable employees as well as the increased influence of internal brand champions.

According to 87% of applicants, would cause them to reconsider a organisation or job, and they are more than twice as likely to endorse a business. Employing solutions that are nimble and driven by people science can assist in recruiting employees that produce the greatest results and significantly increase corporate growth. better performance: Organisations must use internal recruitment to fill crucial positions and skill gaps. Because it empowers them, fosters their growth, and builds their faith in the organisation, internal candidates perform better in their jobs. The first goal must be to mobilise the current workforce by identifying HIPOs and closely observing their development. The most effective and precise method of locating talent worldwide is through virtual evaluations. Because recruiting, succession planning, and development choices are being made more quickly, organisations are increasingly considering revamping their employees management approach.

For the majority of HR managers, increasing DIBE has always been a priority. According to the SHL-Lighthouse analysis, businesses with the greatest results (revenue, employees retention) are more likely to assemble a broad group of stakeholders to support talent mobility efforts. According to a collaborative survey conducted by SHL and Lighthouse, 88% of employees would stay at a organisation longer if there were professional development possibilities. Internal recruiting speeds up onboarding and improves employee engagement. As they remain with the organisation longer, it gives the employees opportunities and helps to lower employee turnover.

The best and most objective talent identification outcomes come from using evidence-based data rather than intuition. Assessments are founded on science and technology, are data-driven, and provide a superior experience while still retaining a human element to the process. This contributes to increased process transparency. More significantly, real-time data access is required to give HR and leaders the information they need to make people-related recruiting, re-deployment, and succession decisions. The third year of the epidemic will be 2022. In the new normal, recruiting managers will have the authority to use objective facts rather than just their opinions when making talent decisions. Because companies succeed when people succeed, the HR departments of the future will use the lessons learned from consumer marketing in their operations to develop effective brand ambassadors from their workforce and have a greater impact on the organisation.

Leaders may understand and develop business excellence from a new viewpoint and improve the health and profitability of their businesses by using the analogy between the human energy system and the organisational energy system. This new mindset represents a fundamental change in business toward more sustainable ways of engaging people and managing our finite resources. I would like to offer such a path in this chapter, by going beyond the traditional, restricted mechanical models of organisations and toward a more fluid and holistic view of organisations and their surroundings. According to me, you must enhance your organisational consciousness. Also, you must learn to behave with a deeper grasp of the current corporate landscape's interconnectedness.

What makes someone a good leader?

Today's leaders mentor and coach rather than micromanage and serve as gatekeepers. Instead of attempting to do everything themselves, they are advocates for their employees and provide them with the tools they need to succeed. They value their workers, give them chances, and share their achievements. Modern leaders naturally foster ties among their employees and are inclusive. By linking workers to these three pillars, contemporary leaders foster personal growth.

"An excellent leader cares about people and uses coaching, mentoring, and listening to bring out the best in them. As the modern leaders are the most effective."

Any performance model that can be applied to a wide range of organisations, focusing on people attitude rather than skills; a process for closing the gap between desired and actual outcomes; how to accelerate performance in real time; exhibiting a set of behaviours that others choose to follow; and avoiding the victory of compliance over outcomes. I would reconstructs the determinants of high performance with uncommon clarity, insight, and accessibility in this chapter, illustrating and explaining concrete tools and strategies that readers may use in their own teams and organisations.

What elements of an organisation's culture can leaders influence?

Every leadership plan should put a lot of emphasis on inspiring people since leaders have a tremendous impact on the culture of a business. There are many ways to do this, but the following are standing out:

- Those in positions of authority must live up to the culture they promote. In the event that confidence is ever betrayed, a sincere apology (and, depending on the circumstances, possibly even repercussions) had best come quickly after. When you take a step back, you might be amazed by how much you can learn.

- They offer a channel for unrestricted dialogue. When everyone has the opportunity to question the top leaders, answers may be provided immediately. In addition to giving employees a voice, this is a wonderful approach to reiterate the organisation's objectives and core values.

- They react to criticism in a meaningful way. The value of requesting feedback is based on the subsequent action. It won't get away with acting like you're listening.
- They give their employees authority. More creative thinking and problem-solving are possible in an autonomous culture. When given the freedom to contribute (with responsibility), employees will perform above and beyond everyone's expectations.
- They keep an eye out for new ideas. It may often be quite instructive to take a step back and observe what's going on in the office. Pay attention to minute details about the workplace and how people behave.
- They assure employees that failure is not deadly. Any person may fail, regardless of who they are. It simply indicates that risks were taken and progress is being made. People should be encouraged to learn from their mistakes and do things better the next time, instead of being punished for attempting.
- They show gratitude for a job well done. Openly expressing gratitude to coworkers makes them happier and more effective. Employees are more committed to their team and the organisation as a whole when they feel that their work counts, that it matters, and that their superiors appreciate what they do.

Myths about the effects of leadership on organisational culture?

It is clearer than ever that the workforce of today needs an efficient, universal leadership style. An organisation's work culture is greatly influenced by the experience, engagement, and wellness of its employees. I've looked at fallacies about how leadership affects corporate culture to help executives decide where to start.

- Interactions between individuals are the only thing that constitute culture. Yes, it's beneficial when individuals can just "get along" with one another. But culture encompasses much more than that; it also considers unstated behavioural rules.
- The culture of an organisation is heavily influenced by factors such as beliefs, clarity, dedication, purpose, and results. An organisation's culture ought to emerge naturally. The norms, relationships, and behaviours seen on a daily basis at an organisation form its culture. This implies that if sound ideas aren't purposefully established as a basis, the wrong kind of culture may emerge more quickly than anticipated.
- Organisation culture cannot be rebuilt by leaders. Poor leadership may result in a broken culture, which excellent leadership can fix and restore. However, new (or enhanced) leaders can more effectively relate to employee members with the shared goal of fostering a friendly, upbeat workplace culture. A culture of appreciation may be established through fostering communication and a sense of success where individuals feel appreciated.
- Hiring, engaging, and growing employees is heavily influenced by an organisation's development trajectory, culture, values, and leadership team. An organisation's ideals are its foundation. Strong roots are required for the formation of any organisation. Even if the organisation has high value, it will not expand and thrive unless it has the suitable environment (culture) in which to do so.

- Having fun is fundamental to culture. Even though "fun" work environments appear to attract a lot of attention, employee benefits and social activities are only so effective. Field excursions will never be able to replace having the proper systems in place, supported by strong leadership, and complemented by positive attitudes.

- Performance is not influenced by organisation culture. There is no getting past the fact that a organisation's culture and performance on almost every benchmark are highly correlated. Employees are more motivated to put in extra effort for their managers when they have faith in them. Success is determined by efficiency and effectiveness, which are influenced by successful leadership.

- HR is in charge of culture. It's a prevalent misperception that corporate culture is solely initiated and fostered by the human resources department. The truth is that for a unified and significant culture to spread, every leader and employee must be on board. Mentoring is useless. Focusing on the growth of those who report to you is one of the most beneficial things a leader can do. Leaders are in a special position to support and guide their teams. Instead of only acting as the doorkeeper to employees' internal careers, organisations should train managers on how to help their employee.

- The yearly evaluation is successful. When done incorrectly, relying only on performance reviews might actually do more harm than good because they don't motivate employees or enhance productivity. Feedback that is timely and useful has become the new norm. Employees of supervisors who give weekly feedback are 5.2 times more likely to agree that they get relevant feedback, 3.2 times more likely to be inspired to produce excellent work, and 2.7 times more likely to be engaged at work, according to Gallup.

- Organisational values are distinct, and defining them effectively necessitates the ideal atmosphere for them to flourish. True principles and the correct culture are what attract talent to an organisation and drive people to stay with it. Simply posting values on a website and in an e-mail signature will not help an organisation retain top talent unless its promoters, leaders, and other stakeholders live up to the specified principles. When an organisation's ideals aren't given the space they need to be put into action, the culture becomes poisonous. As a result, such a culture has curtailed talent's career or affiliation with the organisation.

- Recognition isn't all that significant. Although C-suite executives sometimes struggle to empathise with workers on the front lines, applauding their good work demonstrates the organisation's core beliefs. Recognition programmes are an excellent way to incorporate gratitude into daily work because they hold employees accountable in a constructive manner, regardless of their function. Employee appreciation is irrelevant. Leaders (and peers) have the chance to let workers know their work matters and to demonstrate their value to the organisation via stand-up recognition occasions.

- Regular check-ins offer more of a chance to make sure workers are connecting their job to their mission, identifying chances for growth, and fostering a more meaningful discourse. It is expensive to build a solid culture. Big businesses can spend a lot of money developing and marketing a strong culture, but that doesn't imply that's the only option.

- Time is the largest investment a organisation can make in its culture. Making an effort and being patient will pay off more in the long run. The ultimate result will be better if you put some effort into it and have some patience, rather than just throwing money at the issue.
- Pay increases result in improved cultures. This idea is out of date. While equal pay is vital for a stronger culture, other factors are also very important. Positive chances and relationships, inclusivity, and honesty provide high levels of general contentment.

How Talent Management has been changed by the pandemic globally?

Talent management has been changed by the pandemic. A continuum with two extremes describes it. One is what we refer to as the exclusive approach to talent management, in which you concentrate on a limited number of high-potential workers, most capable employees, and employees who are more valuable in terms of their performance—what they offer to the businesses. The inclusive approach, on the other hand, makes the case that everyone is gifted and should be handled according to their skill set.

In accordance with my theory and the way I teach it, talent management is a branch of human resource management that concentrates on your most important workers. The argument is founded on the exclusive approach, which holds that talent should be handled in accordance with his or her value to the company and that a limited number of really talented individuals in crucial or important roles make distinct contributions to organisational success. similar to Pareto's Principle or the 20/80 rule, which states that 80% of a company's revenue or profit comes from 20% of its employees.

HR is crucial in developing leaders with the right qualities and in keeping the best employees in the company. HR solutions can support HR leaders in creating and managing teams, getting the greatest performance out of them, and contributing to the overall productivity and expansion of the business. The talent management landscape of today is defined by the fact that "change is the only constant" due to shifting worldwide work patterns. Flexibility, work-life balance, and a positive work atmosphere are equally important to young professionals as an alluring compensation package and career chances.

Talent management is a dynamic process that will continue to be a somewhat difficult path ahead in the futre, but it will undoubtedly be an exciting one as well. Let me state the obvious first. The Indian economy and jobs remain difficult as the calendar turns. To combat this climate, it is crucial for leaders to continually engage staff members and communicate the proper message about the organisation's primary objectives and initiatives. Without suggesting any significant changes to the organisation's basic principles and employee-centric policies, this can entail tighter KRAs and process simplification.

Due to the shifting demographics of the global workforce, workplace diversity and inclusion are more of a requirement than a choice. In reality, the shift in demography reveals that a greater share of educated and talented workers, who will also be tomorrow's customers, are coming from developing countries and communities. Therefore, it is crucial that communities develop workplace integration skills and enable everyone to steadily ascend the social and economic pyramid. If your business wants to promote more diversity, you might wish to think about your system's present capabilities and whether or not diversity initiatives are supported by them. Building a broad talent pipeline is crucial since it's sometimes against the law to display preference in hiring. A new technology sector has emerged in response to diversity, inclusion, belonging, and equality (DIBE) challenges to assist enterprises in overcoming weaknesses.

Flexibility, work-life balance, and a positive work atmosphere are equally important to young professionals as an alluring compensation package and career chances. Remote work and team projects are rapidly taking the place of the conventional "office," and smart technology is driving facilities management. The epidemic and how HR directors are reacting to the ensuing new work paradigms have contributed to the newest developments in talent management. I've put together this brief look at the key emerging trends in talent management to help you understand what this exactly means, how to compete for increasingly hard-to-find talent, keep the talent you already have, and make sure your people are engaged and have a clear career path in your organisation.

The HR manager places just as much importance on an employee's financial stability and professional development as they do on their mental and emotional well-being. An open-door policy, which many firms have implemented, will encourage new-age workers to share their thoughts, views, and ideas. Globalisation has become the new standard, and businesses are now engaging with customers both inside and internationally, which requires a solid digital foundation to increase efficiency. If e-commerce was the rage five years ago, artificial intelligence is now (AI).

Leaders must understand that while some employees may still desire to visit the office sometimes, relatively few do so on a daily basis. Flexibility in scheduling will be crucial for occupations that need physical presence; flexible shifts will allow parents to work part-time as instructors; and flexible days will allow the workforce to work in a way that supports life.

To increase workforce flexibility to improve workforce sustainability many businesses included contingent employment in their strategic planning, and many of them even had plans to investigate it before the pandemic became a significant concern. "Workforce" is used to refer to full-time, permanent employees. However, many companies no longer operate in this manner. The epidemic has motivated organisations to speed up their transition, and some will likely shift their employment model permanently.

According to a survey report, businesses are eager to employ both flexible and long-term employees. About 51% of managers have combined internal duties for temporary and permanent employees. As a result, a lot of businesses have also been pushed to think about how to employ talent, curate it, and re-deploy it wherever it is required as a result of the increased interest in direct sourcing of contingent labour. The existing approach does not enable an optimal talent strategy; therefore, firms will also need to consider how they will redefine work to capitalise on the accessibility and flexibility of contingent employees. Leaders and recruiting managers will need to dismantle silos and consider how various work arrangements might provide greater results than standard hires in order to maximise contingent talent.

The given views or thoughts are mostly applicable in an Indian subcontinental setting, while certain components may have worldwide relevance. I have drawn on my personal experience to provide what is essentially an observational kaleidoscope of organisational behavior. The purpose of this book is not to pass judgement, typecast, or categorise organisations. It makes no recommendations and is merely an attempt to expand on a thought process that is already prevalent in corporate circles and attempts to develop an outstanding culture in the organisational environment.

The importance of strategic direction is explained in this book. Understanding your organisation's purpose, its applied metrics, strategic communications, strategic hiring, purposeful culture, relational trust, employee empowerment, and work environment optimisation are all important steps in achieving organisational excellence. This book assesses the prevalent winning culture in selected organisations based in India and across the globe, covering all major business sectors.

The book will be useful to business leaders since it tries to suggest some practical solutions for organisations to improve their current processes. All big organisations have information technology woven into their fabric. From enhancement to assurance of effectiveness, it has evolved into a guiding factor for corporate excellence. Organisational excellence is a long-term competitive advantage that allows a organisation to outlast its competitors. Organisations that have remained good for a long time have some characteristics, such as allocating more resources and attention to particular crucial areas. The topic of key drivers of organisational excellence is timely in the intensely competitive business climate that every organisation in every industry faces. Many businesses are obsessed with metrics, but often neglect to focus on and control performance drivers. It's crucial to understand the difference. Performance is produced by key drivers, and performance is measured by keyindicators.The most important factor is the alignment of the five drivers: organisational culture, strategy, processes, structure, and people.

Effective recruiting strategies minimise employee turnover, lower recruitment expenses, and increase efficiency. Take the time to define the ideal attributes you are looking for in new workers to ensure you pick the right people. These traits will be determined by your organisation's culture as well as the abilities required in your organisation. For example, if your organisation is in need of IT expertise, you must prioritise this in your hiring procedures. While talents are crucial, cultural fit is crucial.

"The secret of living a life of excellence is merely a matter of thinking thoughts of excellence. Really, it's a matter of programming our minds with the kind of information that will set us free."- Charles R. Swindoll

Managing change might feel like navigating a ship into a big storm that your crew can't see. Have you ever been a part of an organisational transformation that was poorly managed? You thought you took the time in your business to fully think through the substantial change you were making to your organisational structure. You prepared, and you had multiple one-on-one meetings. Yes, you made certain decisions, but you then communicated them to all of the top management.

You used a trickle-down technique to disseminate knowledge throughout the business, and you even included opportunities for bottom-up queries and input. Even after all of that, many across teams thought you messed up the transition. Some people jumped overboard, while others called for a mutiny. It's true that it's difficult to please everyone. It's also easy to think that people heard but didn't like the change, or that poor communication wasn't the underlying issue. Perhaps you can relate. But what did you discover? Change, on the other hand, can never be over-communicated.

The use of technology and mobility has had a significant influence on how we manage people and how work is done, much like the majority of other aspects of human resource management. Following COVID, I believe the following conclusions are crucial: The global distribution of talent is facilitated by technology and remote work. Previously, you would bring talent to your work; now, talent may be brought to your work. Through technology, it is now possible to transfer work to talent that is located in another nation or region, develop that skill, and keep that talent. This tendency has been there for some time, but COVID made it stronger.

I've seen that employees now have greater choice over their employment, including where and how they work. If you are a high performer or a high-potential employee, you are in charge of the dialogue. The rules are being set by you. Now, employers pay attention to a organisation's culture. The subject of "what is organisational culture now?" has been debated. If individuals are no longer gathering in the same buildings for meetings, then organisation culture is also shifting and adapting. The characteristics of the new civilisation are yet unknown to us. It is changing. The importance of talent analytics will increase. Every single item is always being measured. The question is, "What should we do with this data?" Data will be used more and more in real-time decisions.

How can businesses sustain a solid culture in a mixed setting?

Implementing culture checks is a wonderful place to start (before it's too late!). The culture of a organisation is frequently disregarded until it starts to poison the workplace. Waiting until employees become disengaged and unmotivated, however, may result in significant time and financial losses for a business, since the culture that an organisation cultivates basically establishes expectations for how new employees will behave and communicate. Additionally, it puts the retention of new hires at risk and fosters a demotivating work atmosphere when new employees join a team that lacks interest. That is how businesses that understand the negative effects of disregarding culture checks keep one step ahead of their rivals by encouraging frequent culture checks and benefiting from having sustainable cultures.

Analysing the current culture is the first step toward change. Then, businesses make sure that everyone is on the same page about the shifting culture. They spot possibilities and holes that are already present. They continually try to see themselves in each employee's position. Better engagement is facilitated by personalising the work experience. The greater picture is constantly at the forefront. Of course, individual contributions are emphasised, but the overall objective is shared, and people start to think as a team instead of waiting for approval from their superiors. Openness, transparency, and inclusion are all hallmarks of HR.

In contrast to "what is the person willing to contribute?" From the leadership perspective, "what is in it for the individual?" Employees are now responsible for actively engaging with their leaders and learning from their mistakes, increasing transparency. On the other hand, leaders engage employees members in a two-way information exchange and give them a sense of importance while discussing their goals, interests, and potential development areas. Such a platform, for every employee, captures the essence of how their organisation adds value to its clients and employees while also fostering an atmosphere that inspires people to explore, learn, develop, and have fun. When used on the correct sort of person, creating an atmosphere that encourages learning through difficulty and time-bound progress has been found to be effective. Value propositions now dominate the workplace instead of perks and compensation. Think about globally shared ideals and values, chances for professional growth, corporate social responsibility, and, when applicable, flexible work schedules.

As a recruiter, one must develop generosity and a genuine interest in othersges learning through difficulty and time-bound progress has been found to be effective. Value propositions now dominate the workplace instead of perks and compensation. Think about globally shared ideals and values, chances for professional growth, corporate social responsibility, and, when applicable, flexible work schedules. When starting a negotiation, focus on areas of agreement. Explain everything in detail, even if you have to reject a candidate.

Understanding and creating experiences that are developmental in nature is a vital component of a leadership development endeavor. While it's obvious that throughout this crisis, the way we operate has changed, our purpose and the importance of leadership haven't. Leadership development approaches will need to change in accordance with the new leadership paradigm, which will call for leaders to be purpose-driven and inspiring via real-time learning from real-world challenges and action learning initiatives. relying on digital resources.

Managing talent in the workplace will become a digital role as digital technologies continue to permeate all facets of professional life. Through effective procedures, cutting-edge technology has the ability to bridge the gap between task management and time management, possibly freeing up crucial time. Such data may be useful in gaining crucial insights into employee behaviour and workplace efficiency, enabling businesses to make changes based on solid facts.

Talent management has often been individual-centered. But because many businesses today structure their work around projects, their employees management techniques are team-centric. Rethinking performance management is necessary in order to support associate-led projects. In order to boost performance, associates should be encouraged to create, carry out, and update their goals together, as well as to adjust to changes and provide new insights. The workforce of today wants more from their jobs than just a salary; they want to work on projects with a higher purpose.

"A talent management plan that supports an employee's desire to make a difference in the world will go a long way toward separating mediocre performance from outstanding performance."

When you evaluated it, you discovered flaws in your procedure. There are certain things you might have done to make the transition less difficult. You know you have a different perspective on management today. So, how do you keep the crew together while you sail through the next storm? So, according to me, you need a tendency toward fast communication. Even if the facts change, providing information as soon as it becomes available and across all roles fosters confidence. What type of communication is required for your team? You must value active communication over passive communication. Face-to-face interactions, small group meetings, and maybe an all-hands gathering are required. Email announcements and weekly memos, as well as displaying information at the water cooler, will not suffice. Change is personal, and you must approach it as such.

What are you going to tell the team now?

You may have heard that, in the lack of information, people make up their own stories. This also holds true for why. When a organisation is going through a transition, you must explain why. Context is essential, and delivering what without the why is akin to offering change without context. You must supply both. Without both, the gossip mill is in full swing. How do you turn it off? Both should be shared.

In any business sector, "purpose-driven leadership" will help to restore employees morale and trust in navigating change for the greatest possible impact on healthcare. The already fierce global talent competition has become much fiercer now that the epidemic has hit. The interview tsunami of 2022 is one of the significant issues that will inevitably arise for organisations throughout the world as a result of this.

The Great Recession's combined difficulties and the COVID workforce shortages are making hiring difficult. The already fierce global talent competition has become much fiercer now that the epidemic has hit. People are relocating and changing employers, positions, and even industries in search of greater compensation, benefits, and a better work-life balance. 40% of respondents to

Microsoft's Work Trend Index 2021 study of over 30,000 employees in 31 countries said they planned to hunt for new employment. Similar proportions of migration were seen in PWC Australia's The Future of Work poll, with 38% of respondents hoping to change jobs over the next 12 months. There will be a greater lack of talent than there was before the COVID epidemic.

In November 2021, the number of open positions hit historic highs, totaling 396,000, according to figures from the Australian Bureau of Statistics. This was 169,000 more job openings than at the beginning of the epidemic, or 74% more. While many organisations have already started the process of digital transformation, we will soon witness a rise in the use and integration of sophisticated TMS throughout the full talent management lifecycle. Never before have businesses employed as many people. Organisations are always in need of high-caliber employees that have the talent and aptitude for their roles. Organisations are reviewing their employees management approach in order to stay competitive in the rapidly evolving workplace. Talent management (TM) is no longer only an operational facet of HR; it is undergoing ongoing change. It is now a crucial component of organisation strategy. The COVID-19 epidemic and recent years have revealed an expanded use of technology in HR.

HR technology is more crucial than ever as procedures like remote/hybrid work and virtual onboarding become the new standard. For a comprehensive approach to the complete employee experience, organisations need to keep up with changes in both the human and digital domains. The talent management software (TMS), an integrated system that incorporates recruitment solutions, learning and management, performance management, planning, and many other functions, was created as a result of technological improvements. While many organisations have already started the process of digital transformation, we will soon witness a rise in the use and integration of sophisticated TMS throughout the full talent management lifecycle.

Today, a range of TM technologies, along with those that are coming to be developed, are assisting HR professionals in being more strategic, more knowledgeable, and managing their largest difficulties. It is no longer appropriate to use a "single system of record" or an "employee self-service (ESS) system." A new set of tools has been developed to build complete employee journeys and deliver a flawless employee experience, boosting culture and employee engagement. The "employee experience platform" industry, a recent development, will soon become a popular area.

Operations are required anywhere. Even once the epidemic is over, there are indications that the trend of remote employment will endure. The future lies in the integration of digital technology to allow people to work, communicate, and deliver from any place, including remote, hybrid, different locations, and time zones. There are now many solutions accessible for working remotely, but soon there will be more improvements. Technology like employee data is evaluated and analysed by augmented analytics to produce more insightful results, identify patterns, and monitor important metrics. The information is then delivered in an approachable, conversational way. It is uncommon for businesses to immediately locate the top candidates for their available positions. To locate potential applicants, HR searches LinkedIn and social media. These platforms, however, are no longer able to meet targeted criteria because they are too big, crowded, and irrelevant. Sector-specific platforms are all the rage for addressing business requirements. These platforms are establishing strong employer-employee relationships and encouraging meaningful interactions, which may help executives locate and attract employees who will fit into the teams and improve the working environment.

Technology and human resource management are interwoven in many ways. The industry, and particularly talent management, is going through a significant transition. Companies that implement these changes and continue to innovate in their human resource management strategies will be better positioned for long-term success. And that process begins with selecting the appropriate technology and solutions that can enhance the employee experience, promote employees engagement, improve diversity in the workplace, retain and recruit employees, boost productivity, and do so much more.

Consider connecting your communication to both the forest and the trees. And it's critical to communicate to your employees why the change is necessary for the business, as well as how it relates to your goal and vision. People are really concerned about how the change will affect their job and their position in your business.It's important to remember that communication is a two-way street. You must listen, and listen some more. It's the old "two ears, one mouth" adage. How can you provide a forum for people to debate and challenge the changes? You could organise a number of participatory, all-hands meetings. You may need to hold small group meetings with the people who will be most affected on a regular basis. In any case, change is a process that must be communicated and managed over time. It's never enough to just make an announcement.

If you're lucky, your team will ask probing questions and raise relevant topics. When the questions start coming, be prepared to listen with empathy. Change may be terrifying. Some people in your organisation will freeze, others will fly, and still others will fight. It is vital that you pay close attention. Recognise each viewpoint with respect, ask clarifying questions, assume positive intent, and most importantly, avoid becoming defensive. It's tough to overcommunicate when it comes to change. I hope you can learn from my mistakes as you traverse these treacherous seas. And, while the process may still have some difficult patches, you'll be more real, transparent, and compassionate, and you'll sail through the tough patches, creating trust with your crew and improving morale.

From the viewpoint of its employees, what makes a organisation great? If ever there was an open-ended inquiry, this is it. The possibilities are nearly unlimited, and it all depends on who you ask. However, if I were to answer this issue in a single statement, it would be that excellent employers know how to keep their employees motivated. Employee involvement is critical to a business's success. Only 34% of the US workforce is said to be engaged, costing $7 trillion in lost output. Here are a few examples of how excellent organisations cherish and respect their employees. If you follow these steps, you'll be the next organisation that everyone wants to work for.

Feedback is really important. It is the key to both trust and vulnerability. But it's more than just soliciting input. Things started to get strange following the request. You began asking that question the very next day, and it profoundly transformed how you interacted with each member of your team over the following three months.

When you posed the question for the first time, the majority of your team requested you to repeat it and stared at you.

Giving feedback back was no longer an option you provided; it was now a must, and it worked, kind of. You didn't get a yes the next week. You begin to receive genuine input, such as what the team wants you to accomplish or refrain from doing. Asking for input is simply the first step. After you've asked, you must listen, which might be a challenging job. You'd want to share a few key things you've learned about getting feedback. First, the quality of feedback you receive is proportional to your level of trust in your reports. Some members of my team offered specific suggestions for how you could better assist them with their work. Others remained ambiguous and safe.

If not, what can you do to build that trust? Creating a secure setting includes all the nonverbal indicators you provide; for example, are you looking straight at the person you're speaking with? Or are you engrossed in your computer? Are you looking at the same thing? Is your body language mimicking theirs? Making these changes will show your direct report that you care about them.

Make a safe space for yourself and be prepared to truly listen. Now comes the difficult part. Don't respond when your direct offers its feedback. If your team is anything like mine, your reports will contain difficult-to-hear information. Some of the input will be accurate, perhaps more than you'd like to accept. You'll also encounter certain misconceptions based on insufficient facts, as well as other concepts that simply don't make sense.

You'll almost certainly be inclined to take all of the comments personally. Take a deep breath, listen, and refrain from reacting. Remember, you asked for criticism;

there's no use in whining now that you're getting it. Make it a point to emphasise that feedback is beneficial. Thank you for being open and honest. For the most stupid or cruel demands, and there will be some, ask for some time to think it over and vow to either modify things or discuss why the change is probably not the best way ahead. The key to navigating this process is to listen for understanding and be prepared to grapple with the comments you hear. This will not only help you and your team build trust, but it will also help you do things that help your team get work done and avoid doing things that don't. If it isn't a win-win situation, I don't know what it is.

"Every step moved in the chess like competition of the world with

Intelligent ideas surely paves the way to achieving excellence

By efforts based on ingenious techniques to see works are done

With efficiency, effectiveness and suitable efforts to complition!"

Creating secure feedback loops and listening carefully are two of the best ways to be clear from the top. Feedback leads to clarity, and clarity aids in the development of connection and trust. Safe feedback loops allow people to communicate truthfully while decreasing the fear of reprisal and the weight of potential wounded sentiments. The formula for building feedback loops is straightforward. Your team requires a method for sharing. It is your responsibility to listen, process, reply, and then listen some more. Creating a safe environment for your employees to discuss might be more difficult, especially if trust has been eroded in your business.

Messages are misheard in low-trust contexts. Consider a dispute between friends in which a misunderstanding compounds matters. Consider the same debate between two coworkers who do not trust one another. If you want a healthy culture in your business, you must establish secure feedback loops. As a result, leadership can stay linked to the entire business and take advantage of chances to explain and re-clarify as needed. To begin, conduct a mental audit of your organisation. What processes do you have in place to encourage positive feedback within your organisation? Consider how higher-level executives obtain accurate information. We're talking about qualitative and quantitative data regarding projects, initiatives, strategy, and culture from lower-level employees. Hopefully, you have a good sense of your own team.

- What about the members of your team's team?
- Have you made room to skip level meetings?
- Do you have access to front-line employees?
- If not, what can you do to modify these circumstances?
- Is it necessary for the team to meet in small groups to exchange ideas or provide feedback?
- Have you found other anonymous methods of collecting input so that employees who feel less comfortable may still feel like they have a voice?

Whatever mechanisms you choose to use, make sure they assist you in creating safe areas for feedback. Openness and communication are required for the creation of successful safe feedback loops. Is your organisation sharing, listening, and responding in a healthy manner over healthy timelines? Set up processes that will encourage increased transparency and communication if they are not already in place. These feedback loops will assist you in staying in touch with the pulse of your organisation.

Because of the magnitude of the problem, time is of the essence, and business is critical to finding a solution. However, corporate strategy must be aligned with a nature-friendly and gender-equal goal that relies only on renewable energy, recovers biodiversity, strives for gender-equal employment practices, and advances toward a completely circular economy.

It may surprise you how often people with good intentions speak in ways that cause uncertainty and distrust within businesses. Trust, like seeds, requires specific circumstances to flourish. This appears to be fertile soil, adequate sunshine, and suitable watering for seeds. Cultivating trust also necessitates the presence of specific structural features, as well as a healthy atmosphere and open relationships. Every business is unique, but one thing that I have observed that helps all organisations create trust is by promoting transparency between levels and functions.

This implies that frontline employees and supervisors require some access to high-level executives, and more communication across functions will aid in the development of trust in very significant ways. You got the right people in the room to tackle the difficult problem by involving a variety of levels and individuals across functions, and by valuing all views, you established trust along the way. With group projects, you cross-pollinate teams. You bring together layers of employees for social gatherings and issue resolution. You also have communications that improve internal communication among workers and volunteers. For building trust through relational equality, these measures are sunlight and irrigation. Working together enhances communication, and communication fosters mutual understanding, which helps the development of trust. Growing trust and openness are dependent on the soil of relational equality. So, how has your organisation's soil fared? Are you structuring work such that people may communicate with others across levels and functions? If not, now is the moment to make a difference.

Spend time together. It takes time to create trust. Your organisation's crew has expanded dramatically during the previous decade. Throughout your expansion, you kept a relatively flat organisational structure. While this model kept all employees connected to the top, it didn't allow for much growth inside departments, and cross-functional collaboration was limited. Longevity made internal advancement difficult, and cross-functional collaboration was uncommon outside of our directors. You opted to make the organisation less flat in the hopes of addressing all of these challenges.

You created a layer of managers, and in your wildest fantasies, you expected this new team to interact and behave similarly to the director team. Hold that thought for a moment. Consider your senior year in high school. What was it like on your first day of freshman year? You knew a few students from each of your classes, but none of your personal buddies were present. A few students spoke up, most of you remained silent, and a few in the rear created a peanut gallery.

You were a long way from a group of trustworthy buddies. You had a group of friends after a few months, but it wasn't until your senior year that our entire class came together, mostly around a common concern that all of this was going to end when you were off to college. But four years is an inordinately long time to wait for trust. Compare it to your water polo experience. Your first two weeks were spent on double days before school even started. By the end of it, you were not only in shape, but you also had a slew of pals who had made it with you. After two and a half decades, you could still converse with those men. Why did you expect the group to act as a team in the absence of sufficient training?

You must foster shared experiences if you want to speed trust development in your team. Isn't it simple? Perhaps you experimented with a few different types of double days for our new management group, and it took some time to locate the best match. You have a few facts to share as you build your own trust boosters. To begin with, acknowledge that not all time is equal. Next, acknowledge that not all labour is created equal. Your employees will easily distinguish between busy tasks and meaningful work. Group projects that build teams must be challenging and significant, with wicked challenges that your organisation must address. Working on these difficulties together will bring up the types of challenges, disagreements, and shared achievements that you experienced. If there is no opportunity to communicate the lessons and influence change, the team will be aware, and the endeavour will fail. So, if you want to increase trust, you'll need to urge your team to spend time together accomplishing challenging but important work.

Because the majority of individuals are not independently affluent, they must work in order to survive. Great employers understand the benefits of providing a decent salary and recognising employees for their contributions to the team. When employees are underpaid, they may perceive themselves as being underappreciated. These repercussions will be reflected in their attitudes towards the organisation, but they are also more widespread. Low salaries, for example, are linked to increased personal stress and disease, both of which can have a direct influence on performance. Great organisations understand that well-paid people are a financial advantage, not a problem.

Great organisations give their employees a steady stream of opportunities to learn, develop, and grow in a variety of ways. Mentoring team members is emphasised, with the goal of encouraging them to continually strive for their own best while taking advantage of teaching moments along the way. Why is it so critical for the employer to take the lead in this situation? Because if you don't keep lifting the bar and providing your team with the means to achieve it, you'll find yourself stuck with a team that is continually wondering whether there's anything better, and more fulfilling, out there. Employee feedback is highly valued. Many businesses claim to respect employee feedback, but few actually do. Great organisations value employee feedback and pay attention to it.

Smart businesses utilise the review process to keep communication lines open. When an employee receives comments on their performance during a review, they should be allowed to provide input about the organisation and their time working there as well. Smart organisations also know how to take criticism in stride and never make an employee fear that providing constructive input would result in bad consequences. Give your employees a vested interest in the organisation. Here's the deal: Employees are paid to execute a job, and they may be doing a fantastic job at it. But why should they expend more effort if they aren't getting paid?

This is why excellent businesses give their employees a stake in their success. Consider quarterly performance incentives, stock options, or profit-sharing arrangements. Employees that are invested in their organisation are more likely to perform at a higher level. Money is a powerful motivator for people to achieve their goals, and it shows them how much they are appreciated. Ascertain that everyone's time is respected. Some businesses make the mistake of believing that your time isn't valued unless you work in a corner office. The fact is that each person of your team deserves to be acknowledged for their time.

Team members should be provided time to work on assignments at their leisure on a daily or weekly basis. This may be catching up on a long-term project they've been neglecting, cleaning or organising their office or another location they're in charge of, or visiting your organisation's professional library to brush up on their abilities. Giving employees some autonomy shows that you trust them to utilize their time wisely and productively, which leads to respect.

If you're the sort that likes to micromanage, this may be challenging because it requires you to relinquish some control. You hired these people, however, because you believed in and valued their abilities. Why not demonstrate them by allowing them to experiment with different ways of doing things? For example, rather than following a one-size-fits-all policy, an employee who encounters a dissatisfied client might use their own judgement to improve the situation. Top employers understand that diversity and innovation are what set them apart. Allowing your employees to do their duties the best way they know how would only limit their originality and brilliance, which would be detrimental to everyone.

This should go without saying, but it's important to mention nevertheless. Great organisations don't wait till the end of the year to congratulate a team member on their achievements. How would your employees know when they're succeeding if you just told them once or twice a year that they're doing a wonderful job? Talent and hard work can be recognised in a variety of ways. Some organisations have an employee of the week or month program, but personal recognition is sometimes the best option. A thank you and a pat on the back are just as valuable, if not more, than their name on the wall.

Employee safety and protection are not a concern for companies that people desire to work for. This entails having a secure work environment and settings that are pleasant to be in. For office occupations, this may entail back-supporting desk chairs and carpeting devoid of snags. Additionally, the organisation's management consider its employees' emotional well-being. They provide comfortable break rooms with facilities that are within their budget, as well as private spaces for nursing moms or team members who wish to have private chats with one another. Being a wonderful place to work is all about treating your employees with respect and recognising them as individuals.It's realising the importance of treating each team member as an equal partner in your organisation's success. Great organisations know how to get things done.

"Desire is the key to motivation, but it's determination and commitment to the unrelenting pursuit of your goal-a commitment to excellence-that will enable you to attain the success you seek."-Mario Andretti

All of the elements of a performance management system are represented by the criteria's process and outcomes categories, which include leadership, strategy, customers, measurement, analysis, knowledge management, workforce, operations, and results. They offer a systems viewpoint, which means they consider integration and alignment throughout a organisation.

- What is their overall strategy?
- How do they come together for that?
- How well do they put these into practise?
- Do they try to comprehend how their consumers' demands are changing?
- How can they create fresh services, goods, and offerings in light of these demands?
- They measure what, exactly? And what methods do they employ to use measurements and analysis to direct improvements?
- How do they motivate and assist the employee to achieve their best? How do they create a productive workplace?
- What are the main work procedures they use to serve their clients? How are these work procedures assessed and improved?
- Are they assessing and enhancing their management strategies?
- What organisational outcomes do they exhibit?
- Do they have a good trend?
- Are they compared to others?
- How do they stack up against the finest in their community or the best in their field?
- Do they track outcomes across all important variables, or just a select few?
- Who and how regularly checks?

I have the great fortune of working with groups and leaders who are committed to carrying out the difficult job of organisational change. As stated in the statement above, not everyone aspires to organisational excellence. But what may be accomplished in the pursuit of revolutionary objectives is simply amazing. Your consumers, employees, and communities will all profit greatly from this.

The task of top management is to keep them all moving forward at the same time. A definite recipe for failure is to focus on one or two of them and let the rest slip.

What are the guiding principles for managing a changing workforce?

How can a hybrid setup be made into a productive environment? How can performance be measured in a meaningful way? Business leaders need to develop solutions to several important issues in the modern workplace. The epidemic has significantly changed how businesses operate in the last couple of years, particularly in terms of how acceptable hybrid work is. According to a Gartner poll, over five out of ten Indian hybrid employees believe that working remotely increases their productivity. According to the report, the two main factors that promote productivity in the hybrid workplace.

Future workplace trends will be controlled by digital nomads, who believe that talent and work can be done anywhere. The essence of job experience has altered as a result. This has led to some crucial questions for corporate executives. How can a hybrid setup be made into a productive environment? How can performance be measured in a meaningful way? How can you encourage your employee to work hard in a flexible setting?

While every organisation has its own learning curve, there are a few key principles that may be very helpful in managing a hybrid workforce that is always changing: An important factor in raising engagement is flexibility. To increase flexibility, we must provide workers the freedom to choose how and when to do their task, provided that they do it within the bounds of an acceptable and fair mandate. Traditional top-down command and control leadership philosophies are out-of-date and ineffective at changing behavior. Instead, the secret sauce in a mixed workforce is a culture of cooperation, deeper participation, and connections built on trust. The organisation has to have faith in its workers' judgement in order to make this possible. Regular check-ins may be helpful, but it's important to fight the impulse to micromanage. An independent workforce fosters collaboration, which is essential to achieving a shared corporate objective. Additionally, this strategy fosters their independence and creativity at the same time.

A hybrid workforce requires annual performance assessments to change to meet their demands. Setting goals for the full year may no longer be feasible, as the epidemic has demonstrated. Instead, performance management must develop into a continuous process with real-time feedback. Additionally, in order to develop a workforce that is prepared for the future, the focus of performance assessments must include bridging any skills gaps in addition to looking at previous performance and output. Employees in the hybrid and remote office models have also put in extra time to ensure business continuity. This has made it more important than ever for leaders to adapt their strategy to consider all facets of the employee experience. Organisations may restore their social capital and develop the united hybrid virtual culture they need for the new normal by realigning and restructuring people's leadership and management in a hybrid virtual environment and fostering interactions between leaders and teams.

Burnout and overwork become a genuine issue in remote working situations due to the lack of a physical barrier between home and the workplace, giving rise to worldwide phenomena like the "great resignation." As a result, it is more important than ever for leaders to strike a balance between short-term employee productivity and long-term wellbeing. Our employee have warmly embraced initiatives like global recharge days, no-meeting Fridays, and virtual yoga sessions. This requires a combination of compassionate action and favourable rules. Leaders must also set an example for workers to follow when it comes to maintaining a healthy work-life balance. This entails establishing reasonable standards for email and text response times as well as proper deference to "off-work" activities. While hybrid workplaces have fundamentally altered the workplace, the core principles of employee involvement and leadership have not changed. The present workplace disruption caused by work-from-anywhere models has made it more important than ever to prioritise hiring, candidate expectations, wages and benefits, and employee retention.

Since they place a strong emphasis on maximising performance and preserving cultural cohesiveness, as well as ensuring that the workforce is resilient and prepared to lead the future, businesses must rely on these leadership fundamentals to empower their workforce. Today, the majority of organisations discuss employee management as a component of their overall strategy. It is an essential strategy for finding, training, and inspiring employees with the abilities and perspectives needed to achieve organisational goals. This paper analyses the variables that have contributed to the global talent shortage and attempts to identify the main enablers in the talent management process. The report also offers suggestions for using talent management to achieve organisational excellence.

The most effective managers are often terrific listeners who reach out proactively to seek feedback and when combined with empathy, inclusive policies, and a dedication to meaningful participation, the appropriate collaboration tools—such as Zoom, Slack, etc.—can be a formidable force.To make sure you have the team's pulse in a hybrid setting, it could even make sense to err on the side of overcommunication. It may be quite illuminating to combine official employee surveys with casual catch-ups. Of course, taking action on the comments as the next step is also important.

Why is it vital to mentor freshly hired employees?

Mentors play an important role in assisting new workers to overcome their inhibitions and obtain answers to all of their inquiries, which helps organisations have engaged employees and, as a result, reduces infant attrition. A planned mentoring programme is critical for every firm because it allows it to have happy and productive staff from day one. Mentors play an important role in assisting new employees in lowering their guard, overcoming their inhibitions, and obtaining answers to all of their inquiries throughout the early stages of their careers. This also contributes to having engaged staff, which helps reduce baby attrition.

New workers feel at ease as their mentors help them find their way around the organisation.

Mentors spend time with their mentees to familiarise them with the system, organisational structure, procedures, corporate regulations, and so on, and to assist new workers in making valuable contributions. An engaged new hire provides value to the firm and is less likely to depart in the first few months. We also co-sponsor technical certification programmes for our staff to help them enhance their abilities. Our goal is to train the workforce in a way that benefits not just us in the long run but also the individuals in their professional development.

How does an effective onboarding mentorship programme come together?

A strong mentorship programme includes mentors who are experienced, empathetic, have an open and honest demeanour, and are well-versed in the company's culture and values. It is critical that the organisation understands what it expects from its mentors. If mentors are mature enough to grasp their function and the company's value proposition, including its numerous rules, procedures, people values, and so on, it will be easier to express expectations to mentees and new hires.

Mentors must also be there when mentees need them to solve problems, assist them, and offer them appropriate solutions or leads. As communication facilitators, we attempt to ensure a free flow of communication throughout the workforce.

What credentials should a mentor have?

We think that a mentor should have five years of overall experience and one year with the organisation in order to grasp the industry as well as the company's values and objectives. A pleasant attitude, being personable, being patient, being trustworthy, and being an attentive listener are some of the personal traits required to be an effective mentor.

How should success be defined in this context?

The mentorship programme must be assessed based on the achievement of the stated goals. Mentors and mentees must sign up for the programme prior to the start date since they must interact and discuss expectations toward similar goals on a frequent basis. These objectives might include, among other things, career development, onboarding personnel that leads to increased productivity, and boosting diversity.

At the same time, it is critical to examine the mentoring program's success and mentee feedback; the mentee's work effectiveness, output in the first week of joining the organisation, and his/her involvement with the company's numerous projects are some of the indications that may help measure success. Mentee development sheets, which include developmental areas and actionable insights, also aid in keeping track of what has been accomplished and what further needs to be addressed for both mentees and mentors. This may be accomplished by doing a periodic pulse check, such as using a simple Google form to collect information from mentors. Finally, a mentor incentive scheme and a project timetable are also beneficial.

What role does leadership play in encouraging employee well-being and wellness? What are some of the projects spearheaded by Providence's leaders?

Leaders must be resilient when leading treks, showing their teams the way, and assisting them along the road to attain every milestone - and there are many. India leadership team enthusiastically promotes workplace well-being and takes responsibility of what that entails for their employees, whether it's no-meeting Fridays or fun wellness challenges. Leaders recognise and respect a caregiver's personal time off and are enthusiastic about any wellness help that staff require. Our country head is a great supporter of mental health and has made it a priority through several live dialogues and interactions with caregivers, as well as ensuring that we as an organisation provide the necessary resources and support systems.

We also have a strong culture of supporting inclusiveness, and our leaders assist to foster an accepting and honest environment in this place. Leaders recognise that wellbeing has a direct influence on engagement, retention, and business performance; wellness is inherent to what we do rather than a nice-to-have emphasis.

- How do you assess the effectiveness of your wellness programmes?
- How are you ensuring that these wellness frameworks result in actual, meaningful, and beneficial change?

Wellness programmes are a blend of experiences and learning for us. When we focus on wellbeing, it encompasses everything from a myriad of advantages to sensitisation on various wellness factors to learning experiences of personal interests, growth, and communal wellness. Creating venues for open discussion about mental health has bolstered our efforts to create a more real workplace. Employee feedback when major programmes are completed, engagement and involvement in campaigns, yearly caregiver feedback surveys that also assess employee satisfaction with our wellness programmes, mental health check-ins, and employee tools to track wellbeing are all part of our impact evaluation.Our efforts to make a real difference stem from keeping interventions simple and relevant to our workforce demographics, whether it's promoting buddy programmes to assist each other achieve or hosting forums to share stories of impact or viewpoint. All of this is used to constantly enhance the health journey that we provide to our caregivers.

Finally, what advise would you provide to CEOs as they prioritise employee well-being? Is it possible for them to balance their personal time, value their health, and, most importantly, be willing to discuss and be sensitive about their own journeys? Leaders may begin dialogues with their teams right away about how each person views well-being and what they value. It must be weaved into every essential coaching dialogue that a leader must drive.

What is the one thing that leaders must do for themselves right away? Given that well-being is so much about practising to assist replicate wellbeing, how leaders function and behave at all times is crucial. It is a lot about how leaders present themselves at work. There is no HR blueprint, and the function is now larger and deeper. We are in the midst of a workplace change, and there is no HR blueprint today, according to the fabless semiconductor company's chief people officer, who adds that the function of HR mechanisms inside organisations is shifting to be wider and deeper than ever before.

Today's employees expect more from their employers in terms of individual flexibility, establishing an inclusive business culture, responding to global events, supporting mental health, and personalising the employee experience. This is a massive undertaking for companies. It is difficult to meet these expectations and future-proof organisations in a climate of unpredictability and fluctuating priorities. If the previous two years have taught me anything, it's that the objective should not be to futureproof the organisation since it's difficult to forecast what kinds of challenges will arise.

- In the aftermath of a large departure of talent and a tight labour market, how are organisations redefining their talent strategy?
- What are your thoughts on the greater change of talent strategies?

Over the previous two years, employees have experienced a phenomenal amount of change and upheaval. Nobody knows where new labour market trends will emerge. Nonetheless, we are aware that employee demands and expectations are evolving significantly. Personal flexibility and wellbeing are also being prioritised. Organisations who recognise this and change their value propositions will thrive. Gimmicks do not work in the long run for recruiting and keeping people. Understand your core values. Create a solid foundation for your company's culture. Listen to your staff and respond truthfully to them. Recognise and praise outstanding effort. In the post-pandemic world, the usage of AI and automation has skyrocketed, and businesses are leveraging next-generation technology to boost productivity and meet rising customer demand and expectations.

How do you envision the influence of next-generation technology in the Human Resources Department, such as AI and automation?

There is a lot of opportunity in the HR arena to use technology and automation to improve service quality and efficiency. We've seen trends toward shared service models, automating regular processes, enabling employee and management self-service, and using predictive modelling to accomplish some fascinating new things, such as recognising potential attrition risk and analysing potential bias in data. Good human-centered design is the most crucial starting point for innovation. What issue are you attempting to resolve? Begin by building a wonderful employee experience and an efficient process, and then look for the tools and systems that will help you do it, not the other way around. Organisations must strike a balance between automation and human engagement. We understand that connection and community are basic needs, and that human connections are critical to creating a culture of inclusion and belonging. If your new recruit solely interacts with a bot, they will find it more difficult to feel welcomed into the organisation, thus it is vital to prioritise the employee experience.

How is the job of human resources changing as a result of remote work habits, an increase in data, and an emphasis on inclusive culture and employee experience?

We are currently through a workplace makeover. There is no HR handbook that we have seen in recent years, and the function of HR inside organisations is shifting to be larger and deeper than ever before. Employees want and demand more from their employers in terms of individual flexibility, creating an inclusive workplace culture, responding to global events, supporting mental health, and personalising the employee experience. To create and implement programmes that have the greatest impact, it is necessary to understand the environment around you, your industry, your business, your organisation, and the range of employee demands. To be a successful business partner and provide relevant advice, you must consistently commit time in all areas.

- What has been your primary priority as a global talent leader in the hybrid work era?
- How do you assess progress?

Keeping our company's ethos of "do the right thing" at the forefront of our minds. To us, this means giving staff with as much flexibility and individualised solutions as possible as we all manage the epidemic and new constraints on individuals/families/communities. Employees require various things at different times, and there is currently no one-size-fits-all answer. This is especially true for a multinational organisation like ours. We track progress through employee experience surveys, inclusion evaluations, focus groups, leadership forums, and frequent performance and development talks. Our capacity to recruit and retain people is also an important measure of our development.

- What are the main problems and possibilities you see in today's workforce up-skilling and re-skilling?
- Can you tell me about your initiatives in this area?

We have a constant demand for elite talent, as do most rising global digital organisations, yet there is a limited supply. Only employing experienced individuals is a poor strategy for long-term growth. We have extensive pathway programmes in which we collaborate with local high schools and colleges to develop STEM skills and give students with employment options in order to excite them about our business and to expand and increase the entire talent pool. This benefits our people who are passionate about their careers and constant learning, while also assisting our company in strengthening fundamental competencies that are crucial to our long-term success.

What role do you play as an HR leader in future-proofing your workforce?

Focus on strengthening organisational resilience and leadership competence so that we are stronger at addressing new and unexpected challenges in innovative ways to move through the change curve faster, and that we have faith in each other and the firm to weather difficult times. If the previous two years have taught me anything, it's that the objective should not be to futureproof the organisation since it's difficult to forecast what kinds of challenges will arise. What are your company's priorities, and how do you ensure that they are in line with employee expectations?

The vast and rapidly expanding Internet of Things field, this is a previously unknown sector that is now a part of everyone's daily life and is predicted to have some of the quickest technological advancements in the industry over the next decade. To face this challenge, we are bringing together some of the most inventive, competent, and creative professionals from across the world. It is critical for me (and other leaders) to grasp our overall company strategy, people trends impacting our area, unique cultural characteristics that provide tailwinds for us, changing employee demands, and the rate at which our organisation can absorb change.

It is critical to communicate often and honestly with workers about what is happening in our market, how our business is doing, and how our customers and products are doing through regular company meetings, town halls, leadership forums, all-hands meetings, the corporate intranet, and other means. This kind of transparency instils confidence in our staff that we are sharing what we can and preparing properly. We also communicate the findings of our engagement surveys, the activities we are taking, and our progress toward people and culture-related goals on a regular basis.

- Where are you and what are you looking for?
- What procedures do you use to communicate important outcomes and collect feedback for advancement?
- Do you have service excellence standards, and does your employee know what they are?
- How much money do you spend on the training of employee at all levels?
- How can you tell if your employee members are engaged?
- What is required of each employee in order for the business to succeed?
- Are employee ambitions in line with the most important objectives for our success as a group?
- Are they aware of the organisation's and their own aims, as well as how they are expected to contribute?
- How effectively do you identify what works so that others may understand what "correct" looks like?
- How does leadership affect the culture of an organisation?

One of the most important foundational elements for creating outstanding corporate cultures is effective leadership. Regardless of position, everyone with power or influence qualifies as a leader, and leaders shape the culture of their organisations. Leaders may keep individuals accountable while also reinforcing ideals. Depending on the leadership style and strategy implementation, this influence over others may be constructive or destructive, but both good and bad leadership will have an impact on and shape the organisational culture at work. Leaders are urged by SHRM to take their time developing an environment where employee members may flourish. Employees and the bottom line suffer when a strong culture isn't developed.

A further challenge is getting individuals to work productively. You conducted a final conference when the whole leadership team, including the president, debated and decided the final ranking of the talents who had been rated highest in earlier sessions, once all of these talent calibration meetings were finished and the candidates calibrated. You may now understand why I mentioned at the outset that this aspect of the procedure was exceedingly difficult. I also mentioned the necessity for preparation in order to successfully plan talent assessment meetings and choose the top people for your business. And you do now.

When you're prepared to conduct your talent calibration meetings, this will presumably be one of the most exciting phases of your top talent program. The actual action starts here, and it may get really fierce at times. Why do you suppose I call the meetings tense? It's because the managers who make the nominations typically bring a lot of emotion to the meetings since they have high expectations for and strong beliefs in the candidates. You must be well-prepared and have the information in order if you intend to lead these sessions yourself. Above all, keep composed and rational when the conversations become heated. Your major objectives should be to have fruitful talks that result in an accurate assessment of your abilities and the identification of top talent for your organisation.

In a talent calibration meeting, all of these considerations would be used to showcase and evaluate the candidate's potential. You now have it. You may successfully submit your nominations if you put a little effort and imagination into the design of your profile. And you're one step closer to developing a worthwhile program to recognise and nurture your best skills. Differentiate between performance and potential. Being able to distinguish between performance and potential in an impartial manner is one of the most difficult and occasionally perplexing parts of evaluating talent. To help you understand the differences between these, let's look at them more closely.

The easiest one is the last one, because almost everyone likes to be thanked for their contributions. Recognising everyone's contribution is difficult. It's easy to concentrate on the top performers and the exceptional home runs, but it's also crucial to acknowledge those who might not immediately jump out. The worker that constantly turns up and completes their task on schedule also merits praise for their dependability. In other words, give praise freely. And make sure that everyone gets credited for their contributions.

The other long-term advantage is that your organisation, especially its leaders, can establish a shared understanding and vocabulary to identify and discuss one of its most important resources, its top talent, through the talent calibration sessions. To get the participants ready for the talent-calibration sessions, you created and delivered targeted training. To give the managers a realistic idea of what to expect, you organized webinars, Q&A sessions, and even made several movies with roleplays of fake calibration conversations. I have to admit that you still didn't fully prepare them. Once they were seated side by side in the room, it was a very different experience.

The culture of the particular group you were meeting with and how well the participants knew the nominees had a big impact on some fascinating group dynamics. Because certain groups were so close-knit, it was difficult for them to distinguish between the talents under consideration because they didn't want to question or irritate the other managers or run the danger of harming the careers of the talents. Some supervisors questioned the talents' qualifications in other groups a little too vehemently. In all instances, I had to stay impartial and intervene to guide the conversations in the right direction. Asking the participants to concentrate more on potential than performance and not whether they personally liked or hated the talent being reviewed was another difficulty for me. They found it far simpler to discuss the talents' past accomplishments or the reasons why they were likeable than to discuss what they may be capable of.

It also greatly increases the severity of your procedure. One talent at a calibration meeting seemed to have more potential than her boss had given her credit for. The manager acknowledged undervaluing her since she was in a crucial position and the manager couldn't afford to lose her when the CEO pressed the issue. After that, you had a constructive conversation about the significance of appropriately identifying abilities that may benefit the organisation as a whole and not holding real talents back. I've given you my example because I want you to understand how it could feel and what effect you might have after doing your calibration meetings effectively.

It's crucial to obtain the appropriate mixture since structuring and managing the nomination process may be a very difficult task. How come, in your opinion? You'll need the right individuals in the mix from the start if you want to operate an efficient top talent program that will discover the employees with the most potential in your organisation. Therefore, there shouldn't be too many or too few of them.

Additionally, by integrating those who don't really jump out as having apparent abilities, it's possible to uncover some hidden gems. Running a successful nomination process is the only way you can do this. Let's see how you can accomplish that. You had to accomplish this manually using spreadsheets since one of the organisations. This may take a long time and will require a lot of work.

However, after you used a system you came up with to arrange the spreadsheets, you were able to retrieve the data quite quickly. And before the nomination season started, you set this up. So, when the nominations began to roll in, you were totally ready. You would have been in trouble if you had waited until the nominations started to come in. You produced a one-page visual biography of each nominee for each nomination you got that contained the most crucial details, such as their tenure with the organisation and in their current position, performance evaluations, and the sorts of projects or cross-functional experience they've worked on.

Prepare yourself to create a top talent program. When the circumstances are ideal and you have executive sponsorship, successfully executing a top talent program will be advantageous to your organisation in many ways. A significant cultural change program was also devised to aid in the implementation of the new plan.

In order to prevent a disruption of operations in these crucial sectors, they lacked a talent pipeline ready to fill these roles swiftly. The terrible experience of lacking top employees at a crucial moment taught the CEO a valuable lesson. He maintained that the creation of a top talent program had to be a component of the attempt to alter the culture, and the business was in a position to pay for it.

Template that fulfills the demands of all businesses since industries and conditions differ substantially. All have agreed on cultural priorities at the top, and these principles are centered on the institution and its goals rather than on individuals. Successful business leaders embody their cultures every day and go out of their way to express them to their employee. Every day, successful organisation executives embody their cultures and go out of their way to communicate their identities to employees and potential new hires. They are clear about their principles and how those values shape and govern their businesses' operations. See?

What does it mean to be a values-driven business?

An ineffectual culture, on the other hand, may pull the organisation and its leadership down. Employee disengagement, high turnover, poor customer relations, and decreased earnings are all instances of how a bad culture may hurt the bottom line. Culture is a hazy phrase that is commonly used to describe a nebulous aspect of a organisation. Despite the fact that there is a vast corpus of academic study on corporate culture, no commonly accepted definition of culture exists.

Rather, the literature provides a variety of perspectives on what organisational culture is. Leadership practices, communication methods, internally dispersed messaging, and corporate festivities are all examples of how organisational culture may manifest itself. Given the complexity of culture, it's not unexpected that words used to describe different cultures differ greatly. Some of the terms commonly used to define cultures include aggressive, customer-focused, imaginative, fun, ethical, research-driven, technology-driven, process-oriented, hierarchical, family-friendly, and risk-taking. Methods of hiring procedures that are effective might help a organisation capitalise on its culture. Hiring has historically concentrated on an applicant's skills, but when a new hire's personality fits that of the organisation, the employee is more likely to deliver better outcomes. The financial industry need a fresh focus on culture in order to attract talent and applicants. People pick occupations based on the corporate culture.

In contrast, ill-fitting hiring and subsequent hasty exits cost between 50 and 150% of the post's annual salary. Unfortunately, approximately one-third of newly recruited employees depart within a year, voluntarily or involuntarily, and this percentage has been progressively rising in recent years. It might be difficult to find employee who will fit in effortlessly. The most common blunder an organisation can make when trying to recruit candidates is to present a false picture of itself. If new recruits realise they have been duped, they will be dissatisfied, most likely leave, and morale will suffer while they are still on the job. Another disadvantage is that individuals are more hesitant to take unpleasant measures towards those who are similar to them.

As a result, mediocre employees who share similar cultural values are more likely to stay in their jobs. Similarly, while an organisation's comfort level is visible when its culture is aligned, too much comfort, according to experts, may lead to groupthink and complacency. During onboarding, newcomers are taught the organisation's value system, standards, and required organisational behaviors.

Employers must assist newcomers in integrating into the organisation's social networks and ensure that they have early employment experiences that promote the culture. Employers can utilise these programs to push workers to perform in ways that are consistent with the organisation's culture and values. If cooperation is a key value, incentives should be focused on teamwork rather than individual accomplishment. Employers can also highlight individuals who best represent the organisation's ideals. Employees who work in environments where there is a lack of cohesiveness and similar goals outperform those who work in environments where there is a lack of cohesion and similar goals.

Performance management systems may have a significant impact on organisation culture by explicitly articulating what is expected of employees and offering a feedback tool that informs employees about right behavior. Conflicting signals about organisation culture can breed distrust and cynicism, which can lead to, or aid in the justification of, activities as harmful as embezzlement. Cultural discrepancies, according to experts, can lead to workers being frustrated, believing management is deceitful, doubting assertions from higher-ups, and being less willing to put up their best effort.

In the process, mediocrity in performance may suffice in many circumstances. I.e., good becoming better is regarded as a positive outcome. What is lost is the vital component of aiming for the "best" or "better than the best," which is a fundamental component of greatness as a human activity.

As a result, good organisations rely heavily on somewhat above-average yet efficient executors. These performers will inevitably be a modest but vital component of the workforce. The Pareto principle will be well proven here, with 20% of the workforce performing 80% of the productive work that has a significant influence on organisational income. Not unexpectedly, the majority of the organisation's revenue will come from 20% of its clients.

Organisations that prioritise excellence as a fundamental value, on the other hand, will have more genius executors than just effective ones. More significantly, they will consistently and superbly perform even when under pressure, with minimal resources, and when all odds are stacked against them. Excellent organisations will automatically develop extraordinary crisis managers who thrive in situations that are out of the ordinary, need deep innovation in thought and practise, and depart from the established SOP.

As a result, business process methodology is constantly reinvented, with productivity actually growing after each crisis. The internal philosophy of these organisations is to "challenge the boundaries," whereas the former is frequently to "limit the challenge" after the targeted goal is completed to a certain degree.

The evidence-based leadership framework is guided by the principles for organisational excellence. When followed to the letter, these principles provide businesses with a roadmap for building a culture of excellence. Set high expectations in order to achieve the desired results while remaining true to your goals and beliefs. Track progress on a continuous basis to obtain results while maintaining an improvement mentality. With much care and attention, serve others. People may be coached to perform at their best at work. In the workplace, pay attention to aspirations and desires. Commit to individual accountability in order to attain corporate objectives. To move the organisation in the right direction, use consistent methods. People understand why what they do is important. Recognise and reward those who collaborate to achieve results.

- To what extent have you established appropriate goals with appropriate accountability and leadership development?
- Do you have a structure and methods in place for managing individual performance, such as recognising strong work and delivering critical feedback on areas of weakness?
- Are executives constantly implementing strategies, procedures, and tools across the organisation?
- What are you up to, and where do you want to go?
- What are your procedures for disseminating important results and seeking feedback for improvement?
- Do you have service excellence standards, and do your employee know what they are?
- How much do you invest in employee development at all levels?
- How can you tell if your employee are engaged?
- What do you expect of each employee to ensure the organisation's success?
- Do employee goals align with the top priority for collective success?
- Do employees understand the organisation's and individuals' goals, as well as how they are expected to contribute?
- How effectively do you recognise what works so that others may see what is right?

To cultivate a high-performing workforce and engage your people, you must change the methods by which you drive performance and build trust. The change away from annual ratings and toward regular check-ins is a fantastic start toward what's known as performance engagement. With fewer forms, no ratings, and no invasive supervision, you will be able to streamline your procedures. You need to spent a lot of time teaching your executives how to get the most out of these tools.

A candidate experience plan should be a top focus as part of the established culture. You may get a lot of information concerning your candidate's experience on the internet. If your applicant experience is terrible, it has a significant influence on the entire brand of your organisation. Take a few minutes to look up your organisation's web reviews and ratings if you haven't already. More than 80% of candidates looked at Glassdoor.com before interviewing, according to an internal poll we conducted at Panasonic, so you should be aware of what's being said about your organisation on social media.

What should you do if you are dissatisfied with your rating? Take action based on what you've learned from the comments you've received online. For example, to guarantee that we communicated with applicants effectively, we modified the way we talked with them drastically. For example, we transformed our interview procedures into high-touch, VIP experiences by drastically altering how we interacted with candidates to guarantee we kept in touch with them throughout the whole interview process. This does not imply that you should resort to high-priced hotels and limos, but rather that you should engage in extensive contact, follow-up, and feedback. It ensures that people who aren't chosen for a job are treated equally to those who are. Complete surveys before, during, and after the process to see what other holes in your procedures need to be addressed.

Let's believe that a commitment to inclusion and diversity is critical to building a place where people want to work. We can actually affect a corporate culture by using the numerous voices of employees with diverse backgrounds, views, and experiences. Invest time in developing recruiting techniques and creating internal community groups as part of your diversity and inclusion plan. Invest effort in developing recruitment methods, internal community groups, and a diversity leadership program as part of your diversity and inclusion plan to not just recruit for the gaps you have, but also to retain top, diverse talent after you employ them.

You've probably noticed that I didn't mention free coffee, massage chairs, happy hour, fitness centers, amazing perks, development/training, or competitive salary. All of these things have their place, and employees appreciate them, but when we asked our employees what kept them coming back to work each day, these items were not among the top answers. Having a fantastic culture, their personal experiences working with their supervisors, how we engage them as a leadership team to enhance their performance, and the diversity and inclusion programs we have in place were all high on the list.

Don't merely aim to be a fantastic place to work; commit to putting in the effort and attention required to make it happen. Concentrate on identifying the organisation's ideal culture before beginning to live it. Simplify the performance engagement process and make it more focused on developing connections between managers and employees so that deep and meaningful conversations can take place. Take action on any negative comments you may have received about your recruitment and interviewing processes in order to enhance the applicant experience and employer brand. Develop diversity and inclusion initiatives that attract people with diverse backgrounds, perspectives, and experiences to your organisation. Make your workplace a place where people come to work because they want to, not because they have to.

Being good isn't enough for companies. Excellence must be the objective of those who wish to be the market's top and timeless option. Organisational greatness is attained through emphasis on culture and strategy. Organisational excellence is a concept used frequently by businesses to express how they attempt to differentiate themselves from one another by putting systems in place to inspire people to better serve consumers. However, there is no pattern for how to carry it out, and organisations, while recognising the need for organisational excellence, have varied approaches to accomplishing it. When it comes to organisational excellence, it is not one system or technique that is superior to another, but rather all systems, operations, organisations, and people must be able to function in unison. To attain organisational excellence, each person must have the critical qualifications to do a task well and be motivated.

Organisations can improve organisational excellence among their employees by designing appropriate training for them, and in order to motivate them, employees must believe that there are clearly defined and transparent processes that determine who gets a pay raise, who gets promoted, and who gets training opportunities. Managers must establish explicit, quantifiable, achievable, reasonable, and time-bound performance objectives for each employee. Companies that give competent employee authority over their activities allow them to fully utilise their abilities, provide input on process changes, and acquire new skills.

Communication problems can quickly arise in a mixed workforce when people operate from various places and at various times. Therefore, it is crucial to guarantee that work is done successfully by having access to the appropriate tools for cooperation and productivity. A hybrid workforce can be managed successfully and, when used properly, can be a genuine benefit with the right tools. In a short amount of time, tools like Zoom have advanced significantly in their ability to connect, interact, and engage with the remote workforce. Organisational culture is further benefited by utilising technology to create more stimulating, entertaining, and creative hubs in the virtual workplace. Such simple, quick-to-implement, and readily integrated solutions help organisations create inclusive workplaces and promote employee collaboration outside of the four walls of the office.

Organisational excellence is the systematic establishment of a framework of standards and procedures that will motivate all employees to contribute to the creation of goods and services that satisfy the needs of customers. Being good is insufficient for companies. Excellence must be the aim for those who wish to be the best and most reliable option on the market. It is possible to excel as an organisation by concentrating on culture and strategy. Team and organisational improvement goals are framed by an organisational scorecard. What does achievement entail? What is important to the group?

Determine the abilities that each employee needs in order to succeed and meet the established objectives. Develop coaching and continuous growth to boost capability. The behaviour that all employees must demonstrate in order to maintain the organisation's high standards of excellence. Non-compliance with these requirements is not tolerated. Processes for systematic reflection and feedback in performance management To direct individual, team, and system performance, set clear expectations, acknowledge good performance, and have discussions. Standardised processes with alignment, short action cycles, improvement tools, tactics, and procedures are consistently used to learn, fix issues, and hardwire new processes and strategies in order to accomplish excellence and important goals.

Accelerators are innovative methods, resources, technologies, and tools that are tested and scaled up to help people accomplish their goals by removing obstacles and enhancing performance. The guiding principles of the evidence-based leadership framework are the principles for organisational excellence. These principles provide businesses with a roadmap for creating an excellent culture when they are faithfully executed.

- The first rule is to strive for excellence. It Means, to get outcomes while upholding your vision and beliefs, set high standards.
- Measure the important things. It means, track your development over time to get outcomes while maintaining an attitude of improvement.
- Create a culture of service. It means, serve others with extreme consideration and care.
- Create leaders who create people. It means, encourage employees to perform at their peak at work.
- Focus on employee engagement. It means, pay attention to workplace ambitions.
- Take responsibility to be dedicated to taking personal responsibility for achieving corporate goals.

- Align behaviours with objectives and values to steer the organisation in the right direction, use consistent methods.
- Communicate with everyone to make people understand the importance of what they do.
- Celebrate success, value it, and show appreciation for those who cooperate to achieve goals.

Do you have a structure and procedures in place for managing employee performance, which includes praising good work and giving constructive criticism for performance gaps?

Businesses must take deliberate steps to support the development of their leaders, and leaders must recognise their role in influencing the culture of their organisations. Effective leadership development goes beyond attending training sessions, expanding your organisational structure, or even selecting candidates that best match your organisation's culture. The greatest method to make sure your organisational culture and leadership culture are positively influencing one another is to develop contemporary leaders. Considering applicants that will contribute new, fresh, and unusual ideas to your team—"adding" something that wasn't there before—is what hiring for culture add entails.

You can establish an organisation of individuals that brings varied abilities, experiences, and views to the table by recruiting for cultural fit, which leads to greater creativity and a stronger, better-performing organisation. Employees who feel involved and informed about critical events and choices are more engaged and driven to perform at their best. In fact, according to a new Harvard Business Review Analytic Services analysis on workplace well-being, openness and transparency from top executives help to foster confidence among employees. Being transparent and vulnerable also contributes to the development of a trusting culture. And one of the most significant factors in a successful workplace culture that attracts and retains people is trust. Make people feel as if they are a part of something important.

While attempts to promote diversity and inclusion are beneficial, belonging goes a step farther. Employees' feelings of safety and belonging may promote communication, cooperation, and alignment, which can lead to increased income. It's not always easy to create a sense of belonging. You may assess and gauge your efforts using employee engagement surveys, in addition to encouraging your employees to be themselves, follow their instincts, and become involved with the rest of their tribe on a daily basis.

Make sure to build your office with a sense of belonging in mind, such as a common area where employees may congregate. Allowing employees to contact one another on a regular basis will assist in building a sense of belonging. Demonstrating that you care about your employee will encourage them to stay with you. Paying employees fairly, demonstrating that you care about their careers, and supporting good work practices, such as avoiding overworking, are just a few examples. These organisational culture examples demonstrate that organisations that have a strong organisational culture are more effective at both keeping skilled employees and recruiting new prospects. These organisations aren't the only ones with successful organisational cultures. Any organisation, large or small, may enhance its workplace culture by recruiting for cultural fit, promoting transparency, cultivating a sense of belonging, and demonstrating appreciation for their employees.

A pleasant workplace can be your cutting-edge advantage because it creates a positive work culture. Your attitude and manner are reflected on your team. Bliss is a virtue that should be flaunted. Your aura in the workplace has a direct impact on your people as a leader. As a result, when you show pleasure and optimism, you're teaching your employees to do the same. Always attempt to convey gratitude and appreciation for the work of your teammates.

Complimenting little accomplishments and praising colleagues in meetings or in an appreciation note may have a significant impact on their morale. Their happiness is truly linked to the awareness that their labor adds value to the organisation. It is your responsibility as a leader to instill a feeling of purpose in your colleagues' work. This will give them a sense of purpose, motivating them to strive even harder. An engaged crew is more productive and willing to go above and beyond to help your organisation flourish. This has a deeper meaning than merely proximity. It takes a team to be successful. If you can't keep your employee pleased, you won't be successful. Speak with them. Learn about their objectives, aspirations, and motivators. When you consider your team as your family first, rather than merely a group of individuals working for you, a positive work culture emerges on its own. It takes more than simply being a leader to be a good leader. It's also about forming a fantastic team and creating a positive work atmosphere. If your employee look forward to coming to work every day, you've accomplished a significant aim. Fostering happy employees is the first step in creating a great corporate culture.

Finally, your employees are the foundation of your business. As a result, it would be beneficial if you looked after your employees. Make certain that none of your employee feels left out. Pay attention to what they're saying. On their birthdays or work anniversaries, surprise them. Try to get to know them on a personal level, and be open and honest with them. Support your employees and go out of your way to help them when they are in need. You can establish a team that can flourish and accomplish anything if you care about your people and help them grow. It's just as important to keep good individuals as it is to hire the right ones. You quickly recognise that the teams you form have promise and can aid your organisation's long-term growth. They contribute to the development of your organisation's culture and are quite useful. On the other hand, keeping these people is difficult. Make every effort to keep them. Please put together the greatest employee retention program you can for them.

A successful business is built on the pillars of (DIBE) diversity, inclusion, belonging, and equality. People who are developing company plans and goals nowadays must also be able to connect with the audience since it is so important to understand the psychology of the client. DIBE makes it feasible to do that. The previous ten years have seen a significant increase in the participation of a gender-diverse and culturally-diverse workforce, notwithstanding earlier modest progress. It began in the west as a neoteric idea and has progressively crept into workplace culture throughout the world. In today's forward-thinking business environment, practically all organisations are actively working to make diversity, inclusion, belonging, and equality (DIBE) a core component of their corporate culture. Additionally, organisations that promote an inclusive environment have seen improvements in overall performance.

Organisational values are not as static as you would believe. It is not sufficient to go through this process once. You'll need to repeat this process on a regular basis so that your team understands what your corporate values are and how they manifest in your workplace. Not sure where to begin? You may put the method to the test by using one of your own values. Write out what it means to you, and then make a list of the behaviours you would like to see. Then it's up to you to figure out how to incorporate such behaviours into your current routine.

"Managing change might feel like navigating a ship into a big storm that your crew can't see. Some people jumped overboard, while others called for a mutiny. When a organisation is going through a transition, you must explain why. Face-to-face interactions, small group meetings, and maybe an all-hands gathering are required. It's important to remember that communication is a two-way street. People are really concerned about how the change will affect their job and their position in your business"

-Dr. Amit Das

CHAPTER THREE

Impact of Organisational Cultural Influence on Achieving Operational Excellence

"Any great leader is aware that the success of his or her business rests not only on a vision and a product but also on the people—their team members—who work tirelessly to implement the vision and create the product. The most prosperous organisations thus promote cultures that enable their employees to prosper and advance."

At the beginning of the epidemic, many quickly shifted to a remote work setting, demonstrating that employees do not always need to be "in the office" to succeed at their employment. This has made it possible for businesses to hire the finest employees from places other than their usual neighborhoods, and not only from those who live locally or are prepared to migrate. This has given rise to a fast-paced potential for making significant changes in corporate culture.

Organisational culture has piqued scholars' interest, with a particular focus on the relationship between culture and organisational performance. However, the link between organisational culture and commercial success, as well as how to attain exceptional performance, remains a mystery. A mediocre culture exists in a organisation that provides the essentials—a fair salary and benefits package, as well as a generally safe working environment. People come to work to earn a living. Profits are stagnant, and there is little innovation. Organisations that fail to offer even these fundamental services have toxic cultures, and this toxicity eventually kills the organisation's potential to prosper.

The organisational culture, which is essential to supporting the successful implementation of a business plan, must also continue to change as the business strategy does. This is a chance for leaders to refocus their organisation on a desirable culture that is driven by leaders, supported at every stage of the employee lifecycle, and made possible by excellent HR. I think the last 24 months of the epidemic have taught us some crucial lessons. In order to accomplish the results they are accountable for delivering, leaders are now required to provide some level of choice and empowerment over how, when, and where their teams and individuals work.

"The work environment is very important in determining how enjoyable work is. It is very important to work with smart guys who have a superior level of intellectual bandwidth and still have softer skills as well"
–Kumar Mangalam Birla

The corporate culture is significantly influenced by leaders. They decide on the schedule, assign tasks, manage, lead, and delegate. Strong leaders provide the people they are in charge of with a sense of direction, direction in life, mentorship, and motivation. The varied workforce of today is changing what it means to be successful on both a personal and professional level. Younger generations, who thrive on greater growth and mentoring, are not responding well to traditional leadership styles and cultures. For instance, according to our study, just 54% of workers say their managers are aware of what they do on the job, only 26% feel their managers promote teamwork, and only 59% feel their managers appreciate them. A crucial link is the one that exists between a leader and an employee. My research also demonstrates that employees will be cut off from other facets of culture if the link is weak or negative.

Continuous periods of experimentation, trial-and-error, adaptation, and agility will be necessary for this. Inflexible and restrictive approaches that are being reintroduced only because they were successful "pre-pandemic" face a significant danger of alienating people and failing to meet their present requirements, values, and expectations. Leading people through difficult times and converting the risk of a "great resignation" into an opportunity for competitive advantage through attracting and retaining the best talent depends on an aligned organisational culture that is delivered by inspiring and engaging leaders and supported by talent management practises that deliver a world-class employee experience. The following are some realistic methods that executives might use to do this inside their organisation:

- A stronger emphasis on caring and inspiring leadership a crucial area of concentration is still building connections that help individuals reach their potential while juggling the demands of business. Leadership that exhibits trust, sincerity, caring, and concern for employees must get more attention as the epidemic spreads.

- Fostering leadership skills through innovation in a remote or hybrid setting organisations should use new tools, technology, and practises to accelerate the development of necessary leadership qualities as pandemic limitations make it difficult to reintroduce individuals to conventional face-to-face learning. Mentorship and coaching are still crucial today.

- Organisations that are establishing the culture necessary to propel their businesses forward on purpose—one that is aligned with strategy, carried out by leaders, and supported by talent management initiatives that benefit both the organisation and its people.

- DIBE(Diversity, Inclusion, Belonging, and Equality) is becoming a vital component of employee experience, recruiting, and retention strategies. Numerous studies have shown how diversity and inclusion affect consumer experience, creativity, corporate success, and a host of other crucial outcomes. To give their all at work, people need to feel at ease.

- It's much more important than previously to listen to employees and respond to their concerns. More than ever, leaders must pay close attention to what their employees have to say and show a strong commitment to acting on it.

This entails asking the appropriate questions at the appropriate times to the appropriate individuals, which can necessitate adjusting the frequency of your employee surveys. Organisations and leadership must concentrate on using the lessons learned during the pandemic's first two years in order to understand what has worked effectively, what may be improved, and how people's motivations and expectations are shifting. It's also critical to consider innovative methods of operation and to avoid harbouring illusions about a return to the status quo. Therefore, it would be foolish for leaders to not allow some level of empowerment and choice in how their teams produce outcomes. The organisations that most successfully realign their culture to support business strategy and alter their employees management procedures to accommodate new ways of working stand to earn a significant competitive edge. Take advantage of this competitive opportunity right away.

There is a gap between how you want work done and how it is actually completed. And it is your responsibility as a leader to bridge the gap. Getting culture to permeate the whole business is really difficult. It necessitates a shared knowledge of your fundamental values and the actions that those core values reflect. But what generally occurs? People grin and nod, and then go about their business as usual.

Are you too cynical?

Consider that you have a completely engaged team that has embraced shared beliefs and habits. Even if you did, behaviour slips, people go back into old patterns, and you end up with two cultures. You've all seen the one that everyone claims defines your organisation and the way employees really get things done. So, how do you go about fixing it? You bridge the gap by eliciting the hidden culture. Talking to your new employees is a fantastic place to start. It might be tough to tell what hidden culture exists in your business since, well, it's hidden.

The way the world operates is changing quickly. Many people want to know what the best organisational approach is for their business. The emphasis of this chapter is on how to handle a hybrid workplace. The four main workforce strategies are as follows. The post-epidemic world's most frequently used tactic is hybrid work, which emerged from the worldwide pandemic.

What are the importance of organisational culture?

The workforce is more engaged when a leader instils the aforementioned facets of culture in a business. Higher employee involvement has several advantages, including:

- Employees that are engaged are dedicated to upholding a standard of excellence. They consequently make wiser choices, pay more attention to details, and approach their task with consideration. The promotion and upkeep of workplace safety can also greatly benefit from similar efforts.
- Employees perform harder and smarter when their employer promotes and supports a healthy work-life balance. Having a better handle on these two crucial aspects of life paves the road for motivation and productivity. Additionally, it reduces absenteeism and fosters loyalty.
- When employees feel appreciated, they value their coworkers, clients, customers, and everyone else they interact with on a daily basis. Soaring sales are certain to follow when extra effort is put into responding to inquiries, addressing concerns, resolving issues, and generally being helpful to people.
- These advantages are all shared by everyone, not just the employer. Employees of businesses that foster such a culture are more likely to remain there over time. Why? When you feel respected, heard, and given the opportunity to progress, there is just no reason to quit.

- With the increase in engagement that underpins these advantages also comes a general increase in profit, as a result of the outstanding productivity that every employee contributes to the organisation.

A hybrid workplace is one in which employees have the freedom to decide how they will work the remaining business days of the week and are only required to visit a physical office four or fewer days a week. Running a hybrid work model might take many different forms, but the concept is always the same. Communication is crucial for businesses using a hybrid workplace, just like it is for companies using remote-first and 100% remote organisational methods. In order to improve cooperation and communication, many hybrid organisations use a virtual office platform because employees seldom, if ever, physically overlap 100% of the time.

Many of us had experienced trapping in this forced work from home (WFH) social experiment during that COVID time, there had been several discussions about the future of work, home working, and hybrid working. There had been numerous advantages to working from home, and many signs point to a hybrid future where most employees will spend a combination of days in the office and at home each week. But not every home is created equal. Many houses don't have reliable internet, enough room for a workstation, ergonomic seats, supportive surroundings, or just enough quiet. The overlap time for employees in the workplace may decrease in a hybrid future when employees work in the office two to three days per week. This means that organisations must strive harder to be more egalitarian in order to support all employees. I think there are a few significant prospects for workplaces in this regard.

There is much more to fostering a diverse and inclusive workplace culture than simply implementing regulations and initiatives. Understanding, respecting, and valuing differences among individuals is diversity; on the other hand, enabling equitable involvement of all workers and making them feel appreciated is inclusion. Both of these concepts must be understood by each employee and must be reflected in the organisation's activities. Given how frequently the phrase "DIBE" is used, it might be simple to overlook the many connotations of each word. Movements for inclusion and diversity in the workplace have grown over the past 20 years. This is mostly caused by the distinctions in human classification that still persist, particularly in the United States. It is clear that the trend for inclusion and diversity, particularly for people of colour, has slowed down over time.

I can recall being asked to repeat the organisation's most recent mission statement at a business conference years ago. They recognised the value of having a single vision and working together to achieve it. Every employee engagement model created both then and now has it at its core. If you ever wonder why employee engagement matters, all you need to do is glance at your financial sheet. This type of widespread employee engagement has a good effect on the future of your organisation.

I have seen that that new employees had the most fresh eyes for seeing the disparity between how a corporation claims work is done and how it is actually done. Talk to your new hires and find out what's puzzling them. Enquire about the procedure, then broaden your team's participation. It is not unusual for cultural habits to evolve, and it is acceptable to make behavioural changes without shifting your shared values. You might choose to pave that new path. Sometimes there's a valid reason to steer folks back down the same routes they've already taken. To obstruct either of the newly constructed paths, you may use huge planters or a seat. This ludicrous narrative is now being translated. Your workers will forge their own paths, ignoring your organisation's stated cultural rules. You must make a decision. Do you allow for evasion? If you do, the author has discovered that pointing it out, being explicit about it, forging a new road, and paving it will assist you in drawing out your hidden culture. If you don't want the new course to continue, you must make that clear as well.

Is there anything you can put in the way, like a planter or a bench, to keep people from taking that path? At the end of the day, whether it's hidden or obvious, work is being done in your business. The idea is to uncover your hidden culture. When you know how two people handle things differently, you can typically obtain what you need from the correct individual at the right moment, but this will come at the cost of the entire. You may witness this happening in your own house. The kids understand that they should ask you for certain things, but for others, they should go to mom. They know precisely where their mother is, but you have other objectives, interests, and preferences. This is a low-stakes version of what might be a high-stakes challenge.

Misalignment costs more than basic things in your job. It can lead to schisms between functions, confusion across layers, and discord between teams.In both situations, misalignment has resulted in severe financial loss and employees termination. This high-stakes variant can cost your organisation money and employees. It also imposes a significant burden on morale and culture. Misalignment in the bottom line leads to confusion and dissatisfaction, and it's your role to keep everyone aligned. Your team cannot just use the same playbook; you must be on the same page. So, how do you encourage alignment? You know they're effective because low-stakes practise leads to high-stakes achievement. And you've seen how these values have borne fruit in my home and at work. Everything is dependent on open and straightforward communication. Isn't it true that it's easier said than done? You must delve deep and get very detailed. Consider your organisation's aims.

When it comes to sharing objectives, are you upfront and honest? Does your team establish and discuss shared goals on a yearly and quarterly basis? Otherwise, it will be difficult for you to identify and allocate tasks, as well as for your employee to prioritise their projects and time. Consider your roles and responsibilities. Are you honest and transparent about who does what and who is ultimately responsible for moving things forward? Do team members understand their roles and what is expected of them? They probably don't know if you're not talking about it.

In bigger companies, you'll need to convey and redeliver a clear knowledge of reporting structures so individuals know where they belong. Finally, consider your unique preferences and triggers. It is also important to be upfront and honest about these matters, both with yourself and with your immediate reports. Your children are more knowledgeable than you about which buttons to press in your home. Identifying your own preferences, personal triggers, worries, and insecurities requires effort, self-reflection, and emotional intelligence. Sharing these with your employee and encouraging them to do the same requires vulnerability.

When you take the time to make this effort, you make clear what everyone already sort of understands. By discussing these topics, you inspire individuals to be direct, honest, and honest about themselves. You create a safer workplace where people don't have to walk around on eggshells and aren't subjected to passive-aggressive tensions. When you just take the time to talk about these things, to discuss organisational goals, to define expectations about roles and duties, to disclose your organisational structure, even if it's in flux, and to be honest about your personal stuff, the author discovered, People feel safer once everything is out in the open, expectations are clear, and trust increases.People can advance in Maslow's hierarchy. And as you go up Maslow's pyramid, your team will perform better, get stronger, and generate more. This is all easier said than done. So, before starting another video, take a moment to ponder alignment. Is your team on the same page as you and your vision? Take into account your own objectives, job, preferences, and personal triggers. Have you been honest and forthright with your team? If not, restart the chat.

"If you are going to achieve excellence in big things, you develop the habit in little matters. Excellence is not an exception, it is a prevailing attitude." -Colin Powell

Getting where you want to go is heavily reliant on knowing where you are now. You discussed your work style, work-life balance, and how you engaged with peers in the past. Essentially, you have created your own norms and cultural expectations. You were able to appreciate those differences and realise what had worked for each other in the past by discussing them with each other before embarking on a new future together. Now, culture is just how people interact with one another. And, if you set out to create a strong corporate culture, you should begin by honouring the past: the way people used to do things. This will necessitate some sensitivity on the part of the team as they recognise and explain their own cultural expectations. However, by being interested, you will be able to identify and focus on common expectations, both positive and unpleasant. Second, identify potential areas for expansion. People aren't particularly good at knowing what they want. Once, Henry Ford stated, "If I had asked people what they wanted, they would have responded with faster horses."

"The reasonable man adapts himself to the world; the unreasonable one persists in trying to adapt the world to himself. Therefore all progress depends on the unreasonable man." - George Bernhard Shaw

The first area of concentration is a well-defined culture. Your employees should come to work because they want to, not because they have to. The organisation's goal, vision, values, and behaviors must all be identified and branded. What is promoted, discouraged, tolerated, and rejected is shaped by this cultural paradigm. The definition of a culture needs a great deal of thought and consideration. Once defined, it must become ingrained in the organisation's DNA. As we began to act on the behaviors we stated we would not allow, trust grew, and workers began to take personal responsibility for ensuring that behavioral concerns were evident.

Your employee will be a lot better at distinguishing between what they've done in the past and what hasn't worked. Draw these concepts so that you may create them with these issues in mind. Write a list of what you want to keep, what you want to get rid of, and what you want to add. List down what your team actually wants to pack on the journey after they've discussed their previous experiences and you've pointed out your team's shared expectations and places for improvement. It's fine to leave some old baggage at the trailhead, especially now that you've acknowledged and articulated it. If you haven't already guessed, this is a team activity. Culture is shared, and the easiest way to inspire buy-in is to create it cooperatively. Are you prepared to begin? Consider the cultural expectations you have from previous work environments and your personal life right now. Make a list of everything.

You may have taken deliberate measures to transform your principles into practise, and you may have made space for employees to practise having fun in specific ways that are still part of their typical work routine. Now, in your organisation, you've probably chosen values that you believe are essential, and you want to implant those values in individuals and teams, which may be extremely difficult to achieve well. So, in order to assist, the author would like to give a brief procedure that you may follow to transition from values to behaviours.

First and foremost, he wants you to understand what your values mean to your team. Values, such as trust, honesty, and teamwork, can mean very different things to different individuals. And when your team lacks a clear understanding of what each of these truly means to the team, putting the value into practise becomes practically difficult. So, first and foremost, take the time to understand exactly what your team believes about each of your fundamental principles. Following that, you'll need to transform each value into a list of behaviours. This will require some creative thinking. Consider how each value manifests itself in your job.

- What does it mean to be respectful in meetings, collaborative projects, and the break room?

- Is it different for clients than it is for employee? And what scenarios are likely to put one's regard to the test?
- How do tough talk and impassioned disagreements vary while being respectful?

Take the time to consider how you intend each value to manifest itself by outlining practical actions that you hope your employee will adopt. Understanding the actions isn't enough. You must now bring them to life in your team. To accomplish so, you must first address the question, what protocols do we need in place to promote, if not assure, that certain behaviours occur more frequently?

But it took some time for me to really grasp what you meant. You had to speak with a large number of team members. You have to extend your understanding of the term. And you discovered that, for you, cooperation entails people working together in a specific way. It's about bringing the proper individuals into the room, appreciating different points of view, bringing out quiet voices, and strengthening our listening skills. You mentioned that working groups are an excellent venue to foster these practises. So open invitations for working groups were necessary to get the relevant folks in the room. You urged working group members to spend their first session defining relational ground rules for how they were going to work together in order to foster varied viewpoints, pull out quiet voices, and increase listening. But you weren't finished yet. And neither will you.

Your cultural ethos informs your sense of social purpose. What about your cultural ethos, though? And knowing what you're truly about, your cultural ethos, will not only help you hire the appropriate people, but it will also help you keep them on goal together. So, how do you persuade people to work together on a mission? It's a lengthy road, but the author offers a few pointers to get you started.

How can you assure the pursuit of greatness in light of today's society, particularly the unsettling culture that is forming?

People who produce and consume, as well as your own personal ideals, strategies, culture, and business principles are all important considerations. Technological advancements are used to benefit processes and people, responsible resource management, society, and the environment. Having a clear vision that is supported by the shareholders and shared with the team, being aware of the business and market dynamics, capturing opportunities, mitigating threats, creating competitive advantage, and finally, building the foundation of efficiency and effectiveness of any strategy implementation, which are related to: Teamwork that is skillful and entrepreneurial, as well as value-based decisions They are the cornerstone of the organisation's survival.

Is your organisation culture a true reflection of your employees', customers', vendors', and community's experiences? If not, what can you do to change your organisation's culture and align it with its core values? Human resources may detect areas of concern like high employee turnover, low engagement, and diminishing work quality by analysing key HR data. High employees turnover, poor engagement, and diminishing work quality may all be addressed with a cultural reform. In order to prosper in uncertain times, a organisation must focus on having a revolutionary influence on the market it serves. Setting a high standard in terms of how the organisation accepts its social duty and prepares employees to take on a brighter future is one example of this.

In a nutshell, workplace culture refers to your organisation's beliefs, values, and habits. Employee engagement, employee satisfaction, happiness at work, compensation, benefits, and other workplace perks are just a few of the factors that define and assess the health of a workplace culture. Individual aspects are often confused with defining a culture. There are several components to a good and thriving workplace culture. You can't ascend to the highest rungs of Maslow's hierarchy of requirements without first addressing fundamental needs.

A good culture is one in which a organisation goes above and beyond by providing additional benefits and taking measures to ensure that its employees are engaged and connected. Their employee are aware of the organisation's objective and feel connected to it as well as to one another.

In terms of employee relations, these businesses concentrate on and adhere to the law. It's important to remember that a healthy culture is also a pleasant culture. It is a common myth that in order to be drama-free, you must eliminate all forms of entertainment and amusement. But who wants to work in a place like that? A healthy, inclusive, and respectful culture should also be fun.

The roots of a negative work culture acknowledging the core reasons for drama is just as crucial as identifying and recognising it (ideally early, when it may still be readily handled). Any one of these scenarios, let alone a combination of them, has the ability to destroy your business. Genuine leadership The idea that management is hypocritical, that they merely speak the talk but don't walk the walk, is created or perpetuated by a lack of authenticity. Employees lose enthusiasm for their employment, passion for what the organisation represents, and, most dangerously, trust in this climate.

Culture defines all elements of an organisation, including internal and external interactions, in the information system implementation planning strategy. It's crucial to strike a balance between the intended and undesirable effects while encoding and decoding data. As a result, while analysing performance based on feedback, it's critical to treat the voluntarily information with caution in order to foster trust and secrecy, which are at the pinnacle of organisational behaviour.

Healthy cultures may be found in all outstanding organisations. Simply said, your corporate culture is the way you work together. For better or worse, the total of your team's values and actions will colour it. Great organisations are built on a strong culture. So, by enhancing culture, you will increase communication, raise morale, and encourage trust. If your organisation is like others, you've witnessed culture emerge organically. It's probable that you haven't spent the necessary time building it, and culture will flourish with or without your attention.

Cultivating the desired culture is a bit more challenging. You are a organisation that serves around 100,000 people every year and has nearly 500 employees. It's a major thing to figure out how to work together, how to be a team, and how to respect one another. Companies are eager to find methods to distinguish themselves, to position themselves as desirable employers, and to promote themselves as organisations deserving of victory in the battle for talent. Calls for a vibrant workplace culture to be the secret weapon in making all of this a reality abound. In corporate the term "workplace culture" has become commonplace.

Despite all of the hype about how important culture is, few organisations truly put in the effort to create and maintain a healthy and productive work environment. Although research shows that a healthy culture improves organisation performance, little emphasis is devoted to how to build and maintain a healthy culture.

Cultural transformation is, in some respects, the most difficult aspect of organisation transformation. Corporate cultures tend to develop spontaneously, influenced by the personalities of executives and how they are rewarded and acknowledged. Changing a organisation's culture takes far longer than other types of transformations, in part because it's more difficult to transfer ideas and intentions into action and practice. When it comes to the subject of managerial transformation, it likewise seldom happens in a vacuum and has a considerably greater success rate. Success requires a clear vision, dedication to that goal, and practice confirming it.

The common beliefs, attitudes, and behaviours of an organisation and its employees are referred to as organisation culture. Honesty, self-improvement, and communication may be among a organisation's basic principles. A organisation's culture is influenced by a variety of factors, including communication, style of management, benefits, traditions, transparency. You may be more involved, contented, and productive if you work for a organisation that has a great corporate culture or values and attitudes that you share. Managers trust their employees to work hard and make excellent decisions in healthy work environments. Employees trust organisation leaders to assist and encourage them, and coworkers trust each other to strive toward common goals. A reliable group is driven to work hard and is involved in and happy with their task. Employees in a fair workplace believe they are compensated fairly and have the same opportunities as their coworkers. In a organisation that values justice, employees are also less likely to face politics, bias, and favouritism. If an organisation treats everyone equally and fairly, employees are more inclined to operate as a team. Open communication fosters workplace trust and avoids misunderstandings. The following are signs of successful and transparent communication.

When it comes to product creation, excellent organisations will almost always do it based on need (or market demand). For example, if a client or market conforms to a specified product standard, the organisation is required to satisfy it in order to compete in the market. Excellent organisations, on the other hand, will envisage tomorrow's market today, i.e., look forward and produce a product that can take over the market in the future through unique creation and R&D (from the ground up). They will be technological leaders who will steer the market in their preferred path. Good organisations are generally followers who, seeing the potential offered by the leader, take a "me too" approach to goods and business.

What must be emphasised here is that brilliance comes at a cost and is supported by strict work discipline and systematic execution. Organisations that swear by perfection operate on the 100 percent concept, which states that every single default or deviation necessitates a complete revamp of systems and procedures. The primary organisational idea is that greatness is founded on good work technique that allows for performance repeatability. Because of this emphasis on accuracy and consistency of top-tier performance, good businesses are frequently viewed as being either sales-driven or technology-led. Other functions, including production, logistics, and procurement, must, of course, toe the line in order to stay on track with the bigger corporate goal.

How excellent working culture can be rewarding for organisations?

Ensure that your employees are acknowledged for their achievements, that they are regarded as colleagues rather than subordinates, and that they have the resources they need to execute their tasks efficiently. To put it another way, they create a social environment in which they can thrive. Employees who are healthy, especially those who have a high overall sense of well-being, are more likely to perform well at work. And, of course, when an organisation's employee work effectively together, the result is great organisational performance.

Then there are the businesses with wonderful work environments. The success of these businesses may be attributed to three factors: Because culture refers to the conventions that govern how people approach issues and generate solutions, these organisations regard preventing, managing, and overcoming conflict as an important component of their culture. And the outcomes are undeniable: a cohesive and collaborative workplace that fosters creativity and, as study after study has demonstrated, improves sales and profits.

As you have seen in this book, it is critical to invest in the awareness of people who will shape the organisational culture into a more balanced, just, and human one and whose vision, values, culture, and processes will be used to create meaning and value for its stakeholders in order to ensure the search for excellence continues. Furthermore, in times of change, it is critical to decentralise the development of corporate strategies, raising the level of commitment at all levels of the organisation while orchestrating the harmonious implementation of these strategies. Finally, to achieve extraordinary results, resilience is essential.

Leadership, culture, and the pursuit of greatness: In theory, every business strives to achieve excellence, some more than others. Where businesses truly differ is not in their pursuit of greatness, but in how they build strategies to achieve it. There are three ways to consider. While some businesses will attempt to implement two or three of these techniques, only one will often become their major emphasis. Organisations strive for greatness using a conventional approach, an aggressive approach, or a constructive approach.

"Trust is like the air we breathe – when it's present, nobody really notices; when it's absent, everybody notices."
-Warren Buffett

The foundation of any business is trust. It is the foundation of any human relationship: engagement, communication, initiative, professional effort, and even any strategic objective you must complete. Social groups cannot function properly without it.

Without trust, you'll end up with a broken organisation with slow-moving teams. A organisation with a low level of trust is like a jet without gasoline. You may fumble around in it as much as you like, but it will not get you to your destination. Every initiative, job endeavor, and strategic requirement you must complete requires faith in someone. Social groups cannot function properly without it.Without trust, you'll end up with a broken organisation with slow-moving teams. Because trust allows an organisation to function as it should, it leads to excellent performance. It's the first line of defense against dysfunction and the first step toward improved results.

Many people would not say "trusting" or "trusted" as the first word that comes to mind when asked to define their corporate culture. While we may work in pleasant locations with pleasant coworkers, the organisational culture generated by leaders is frequently viewed in a totally different light. According to the Edelman Trust Barometer 2019, trust in organisations has increased to 58% (trust in my employer for information). While this is encouraging news, there is still work to be done to unlock the productivity locked up in organisations, and leaders and managers play a key role. Let's look at how enhanced trust might help an organisation using the example of flexible working. We've seen a lot of companies establish flexible working arrangements, only to have them fail miserably. The first element of this that you must address is generating meaningful dialogues that increase goal and expectation clarity, and the second is developing meaningful connections that strengthen people's trust. When these two things happen, you have a trusting workplace in which individuals may work as they see fit, producing the job that is anticipated without the need for continual "policing." For many leaders, the task isn't as easy as finding individuals they can trust, though that is critical.

"Excellent organisations are relationship-driven and socially connected"

According to Fast Firm, a Fortune 500 organisation discovered that implementing change takes an average of 89 weeks, with 39 of those weeks being a direct result of distrust. You've probably worked in a location where people's work and emotions were unreliable, insufficient, disloyal, uncommunicative, and inconsistent.There will be occasions when you must make difficult judgments. This isn't something you should try to brush under the rug. Let them know that things might have to change and that you'll handle it professionally and compassionately. It's easy to get caught up in the trap of putting others down. For example, you might say things about them to their coworkers. If you see yourself doing this, make a mental note of it and be aware of it in the future.

If you want to take it a step further, have your employees tell you when they believe you are putting them down. Sitting around reading and studying, let alone meeting up with someone over coffee, may be considered unproductive in some workplaces (outside of your break times). Going out for coffee and catching up with someone, on the other hand, may provide more value than we realise. You may be aware that spending time getting to know someone may give us a sense of assurance about them, according to Paul Zak's groundbreaking study into the neurobiology of trust. This causes oxytocin to be released, laying the groundwork for a trusting connection. Finding the "hooks" that bind us is crucial to forging lasting connections. You're all the same in some manner, whether it's our way of life, upbringing, education, or profession—we're all alike on some level.

It's easy to get caught up in the trap of putting others down. For example, you might say things about them to their coworkers. If you see yourself doing this, make a mental note of it and be aware of it in the future. If you want to take it a step further, have your employees tell you when they believe you are putting them down. Assuming they haven't breached the law, you should make a point of sticking up for the team and fighting your corner. This is especially true when they are under duress. It takes guts, but it will earn you a lot of respect. It's what I call a low-trust workplace, and it can make everyone feel extremely stressed and unwelcome. People begin to take responsibility for their duties, assist one another, speak well of one another, interact more frequently, and are more productive when trust is prevalent. People may discuss their challenges and goals in a secure environment, allowing them to attain their full potential as individuals and as a group. So, as a leader, how can you foster a culture of trust?

"You cannot prevent a major catastrophe, but you can build an organisation that is battle ready, that has high morale and has also been through a crisis, knows how to behave, trusts itself and where people trust one another. In military training, the first rule is to instill soldier with trust in their officers because without trust they won't fight."

-Peter Drucker

I will provide multiple aspects of trust in this piece so you can boost your team's morale. As a leader, you understand how critical it is to instill trust in yourself and your team. For leaders, cultivating a culture of trust is a difficult task. When you're attempting to make a change, the task becomes considerably more difficult. The way you treat individuals should not be determined by their position or influence. Good leaders understand that treating everyone equally and respectfully is an important component of building a trusting atmosphere. The great majority of individuals put in a lot of time at work and want to make a difference. People closest to the point of delivery are often the ones who perceive the most opportunities for improving working procedures or providing a far better service. Actively listen and show genuine interest. Give constructive criticism and positive comments frequently so that others understand where you're coming from and what you anticipate.

You may also be transparent by owning up to your faults and being vulnerable in front of others. This demonstrates that you're not flawless, and it's a terrific approach to demonstrate that others can trust you. Your employees will learn to be more candid with you and one another if you set an example for them. Respect does not require you to agree with everyone. However, honoring their feelings fosters trust, which allows them to open up more freely. Respect is only the application of the Golden Rule: "Do unto others as you would have them do unto you." Let me offer some data on organisational trust that you should be aware of. One in three individuals do not trust their employer, according to the latest Edelman "Trust Barometer" (a poll of 33,000 people in 28 countries). They also observed that from the highest to the lowest levels, trust diminishes. For example, 64% of executives trust their companies, compared to 51% of managers and 48% of other employees. Employees stated that they trust their peers more than their organisation's CEO and upper-level executives. That implies that the higher you rise, the more important it becomes to establish trust with people below you. Leaders are at the forefront of building trust. Give them a task that they must complete as a group. If they fail, they will all bear the consequences. If they succeed, they will all be rewarded. A team that suffers and triumphs together stays together.

Leadership guru John C. Maxwell remarked, "People don't care how much you know until they know how much you care." When someone realizes that you regard them as a person and not simply as an employee, trust is developed. You can show people you care about them by learning more about them, expressing your appreciation to them on a regular basis, and asking for their opinions more frequently.When individuals feel appreciated, you acquire not just their trust, but also their loyalty.

"Trust is the antidote that overcomes fear – and fear is the greatest inhibitor of all to a relationship that welcomes and nurtures new ideas." -John Pepper, Disney Chairman

It has been proven that people who love their coworkers are happier and more productive—and this does not happen by chance. Providing activities focused on creating trust in teams is one approach to increase morale and create trust at the same time. When comparing a high-trust to a low-trust work environment, the leader's "TRUST" components will either be present or absent. My challenge to you is to work on establishing one of the aspects of trust every day. Today, work on being transparent; tomorrow, work on showing others respect; and so on. Continue until you've established a high-trust work atmosphere and increased workplace respect.

It's simple to claim that you trust your employees, but do you really? Do your actions demonstrate your belief that your employees will do a good job or make the best decisions? While many leaders claim to trust their employees, my experience as a consultant for complex organisations has taught me a different aspect.

A lack of trust fosters emotions of powerlessness and dissatisfaction, which lead to a lack of effort and caring. According to research, 96% of engaged employees trust management, compared to 46% of disengaged employees. It's an indication of a good workplace atmosphere if you trust your colleagues and they trust you back. Collaboration and total control are just not possible for leaders. People must feel comfortable sharing their opinions and cooperating with one another in order for your business to thrive. Employees and executives attribute 86% of workplace failures to a lack of teamwork or open communication.

According to PwC, 55% of CEOs think that a lack of trust is the most serious danger to their organisation, yet few take steps to repair it. Trusting your employees might be intimidating; all of the "what if" situations in your head may make you want to take command. But I urge you to pause, take a breath, and consider how simply believing in your employees might enhance your business practices and performance. People who work in high-trust firms have 74% less stress, 50% higher productivity, 13% fewer sick days, 40% less burnout, and 76% higher engagement, according to research. It's logical. Why would you want to work for a organisation that didn't value your abilities, knowledge, and experience?

This strategy is used by Google, and they have a program known as the 20% rule. Employees at Google are expected to spend 80% of their time on duties allocated to them and 20% of their time exploring fresh and inventive ideas. Not only is Google empowering its employees by believing in their ability, but it has also resulted in some fantastic ideas like AdSense, Google News, and Gmail. While this guideline may not be available in every organisations, the notion is what is important. Great things may happen if you trust your employees and have an open communication system. This will help your organisation progress and flourish.

Empowerment comes from trust. Giving your employees your whole trust and believing in their ability to perform distinguishes a bunch of individuals from a team. Giving your employees your trust does not imply that everything will go according to plan; rather, by creating a collaborative and community-focused atmosphere, your team will be able to address difficulties faster and without fear of retribution. In fact, 97% of employees and executives feel that a team's lack of alignment has an influence on the job or project's outcome. The foundation of a great team environment is trust.

Employees' fear of responsibility is removed when you trust your team and develop a community culture. The fear of being blamed can cause anxiety and have a negative influence on employee productivity and happiness. With 56% of employees reporting that anxiety at work has a negative impact on their job performance, this is an area where leaders should strive to improve. Removing the concept of individual failures and replacing them with the concept of team failures is a simple way to accomplish this. If something goes wrong, it's because of the team, so a joint solution may be developed. Problems can be discovered sooner, and solutions can be found faster, if responsibility is shifted from an individualistic logic to a team mentality. This is when trust comes into play.

Similarly, by consistently offering positive feedback that recognizes employees' accomplishments, trust and a team relationship may be developed. According to a WorkHuman Research Institute poll, 82% of employees who had their achievements recognised by their bosses trusted them. Recognising employees' accomplishments not only motivates them to strive even more, but it also makes them feel connected. As a leader, you often convey your team's work to stakeholders and other employees. It's vital at this point to acknowledge everyone's work rather than take unnecessary credit. Allowing your employees to shine both inside and outside will guarantee that they remain devoted and loyal to you and the organisation's ultimate goals.

In all aspects of leadership, trust is essential. It's crucial to have faith in your employees if you want to have a productive and effective workplace. Employee empowerment stems from your conviction in their skills, which simplifies all aspects of your organisation and allows for genuine transformation. Building reciprocal trustworthy connections is how leaders and organisations grow, from ensuring a friendly environment to looking after yourself and your health. I believe it is past time for all leaders to try to change the statistic that just one out of every three employees trusts their boss and to foster a safe and open working atmosphere.

Building trust is dependent on mutual support, and mutual support necessitates both parties asking for assistance. Asking for aid necessitates vulnerability, and when it comes to vulnerability, it's up to you as the leader to make the first move, right? Perhaps you have a few pointers to help you create trust by asking for assistance. First and foremost, do not submit a phoney request. This may sound obvious, but if you don't want to be vulnerable, you'll try to make a phoney request because it's going to feel safer. The issue is that fake vulnerability is unsightly. Consider asking for help where you truly need it, and then identify someone on your team who can assist you. Next, make a precise and relevant request. Being precise allows people to provide actual and meaningful support, and trust is built by asking for that meaningful aid. Finally, don't seek assistance from someone who is unable to assist you. Yes, you've seen this manoeuvre before. You want to give the impression that you're vulnerable. So you requested assistance with a really challenging situation. And the people you ask are ill-equipped to assist. This is like admitting you need help, but it's with an issue you're not intelligent enough to solve. Instead, seek assistance from those who are qualified to do so. You will receive genuine assistance. You'll also hasten the process of establishing confidence. This may appear to be a small matter, but the power of asking for aid is crucial to establishing confidence. Today is a good day to ask for aid.

"Trust is the lubrication that makes it possible for organisations to work." -Warren Bennis

You establish trust by taking concrete actions to increase your team's social capital. You'll find a few suggestions below to get you started. To begin with, it is critical to emphasise that you must always take the first step. You're the boss. That indicates you have the authority and must make the first move. What will it resemble? That is all up to you. Consider limiting shop chatter. When it comes to appreciating individuals, it's critical to look beyond their employment. This has been quite challenging for you. You simply enjoy being there. You just enjoy being on a mission with others. So, while working around the clock makes sense for you, it does not make sense for everyone else. If you want to create trust with your team, treat them as individuals rather than as workers.

Can you take a lunch break, a coffee break, a happy hour, or the first 10 minutes of your next one-on-one? Empathy is fostered via personal sharing. People see each other more clearly as they get to know one another. This, in turn, promotes care. Allow yourself to be vulnerable. Personal sharing necessitates a degree of vulnerability, which may be difficult to do. You've undoubtedly all met someone who overshares, but initiating the discussion is critical. Perhaps you could discuss an embarrassing experience or a personal failing that relates to your current situation. Others tend to follow you when you wade into the rivers of vulnerability. Building social capital will force you to include your employees in all aspects of life. Perhaps you've excelled at putting work marbles in the jar. What about your own personal marbles? If this is already your regular, that's fantastic. Is this a challenge for your team members? How can you persuade people to share personal information with you?

"Those who attain any excellence commonly spend their life in one pursuit, for excellence is not often granted on easier terms." - Samuel Johnson

Do you consider helpfulness to be something that is given or received? Which is more vulnerable, providing aid or asking for it? Requesting and getting assistance promotes vulnerability and support. It also fosters a sense of reciprocity and team buy-in. You used to think of aid almost solely as something you gave to others. You've had a rather wealthy upbringing, and you've adopted cultural beliefs that emphasise things like perseverance and self-reliance. You are frequently eager to provide assistance, but you are hesitant to seek it yourself. However, this is only half the tale. Do you consider helpfulness to be something that is given or received? Which is more vulnerable, providing aid or asking for it? Requesting and getting assistance promotes vulnerability and support. It also fosters a sense of reciprocity and team buy-in. You used to think of aid almost solely as something you gave to others. You've had a rather wealthy upbringing, and you've adopted cultural beliefs that emphasise things like perseverance and self-reliance. You are frequently eager to provide assistance, but you are hesitant to seek it yourself. However, this is only half the tale. Over the last decade, you've become more adept at asking for assistance, and learning to accept assistance has significantly altered your relationships. It may seem paradoxical, but if you want to create trust, you must ask for assistance.

"Excellence is not an easy joke, if one has such an
aspiration as
That needs, ideas, intelligent efforts and alert mind in
works!"

You frequently take disparate pieces of information and weave them together in a way that best fits your point of view. Unfortunately, this contains your prejudices, concerns, and fears, and it seldom casts them in the best light imaginable. What would happen if you assumed your coworkers were trying their best? What if you thought somebody had good intentions even when it didn't seem like it? You feel that this is one of the keys to fostering a positive culture in your organisation. When you and your team start treating each other as if everyone is acting with good intentions, you promote inquiry and understanding over blame and judgement.

In practise, how does this look? You'll most likely need to develop some new behaviours. When your team has issues, they must first go directly to the source. That means no more backchannel chats, no more rant sessions, and no more gossip circles. Your team will need to be liberal with their inquiries. This is curiosity that suspends judgement in the hopes of receiving a sensible response. What if your coworker is unaware that they have insulted you? What if your manager had excellent reasons for avoiding passing on information you believed you needed? What if your report had the greatest of intentions when it inadvertently stomped on a colleague's toes, making you appear bad? However, if you add empathy to the mix, you'll be able to look at a weak argument or a bad conclusion and envisage the finest possible version of that viewpoint.

You'll be able to see the choice through the eyes of the decider rather than your own. Finally, a suggestion. You'll find yourself in circumstances when it's obvious that the individual who is irritated with you did not act with good intentions. However, even in this case, assuming positive intent will assist you in moving forward in a positive manner. This is a method that is effective even though it should not be. So, are you ready to begin? Consider a coworker who has recently irritated you and rethink the entire exchange from their point of view.

Consider the finest of them. Assume your coworker tried their best and had the finest intentions. Then, jot out a few honest, non-judgmental, and forward-thinking questions to ask that colleague in order to truly grasp what happened and to open the door to feedback. The majority of employees claim that they do not receive adequate feedback. When most supervisors offer it, employees respond with argumentative defensiveness. That's why the vast majority of you shun feedback like the plague. Don't, don't, don't do it. It is vital to provide clear and timely feedback to your direct reports in order to maintain successful working relationships. It's impossible to avoid.

So, how do you go about approaching it constructively? The author suggests using the 10x encouragement model. Every item of negative input should be surrounded by ten times the amount of positive feedback. When providing feedback, you must have relational equity to invest in. Now, this may require some rephrasing, so the author has a few suggestions for you. To begin with, keep in mind that your direct report is doing admirably on a variety of critical responsibilities every day. That is most likely why you looked for, hired, trained, and continue to employ that person.Reframe your perception of feedback. Every day, you must catch your employees doing something positive. And when you do, give straightforward, positive comments. Whether the feedback is favourable or negative, you propose that it be delivered in the same manner. Ask permission, provide comments, confirm understanding, and then move away.

Set a goal for the dialogue and affirm mutual respect. What are you attempting to achieve? You and the employee have a chance to join forces and work together to solve the current problem. When mutual respect is maintained, it may be a reassuring moment.Remember that every stress contains an opportunity for understanding. Consider what you could learn from the employee and this interaction. Arrive inquisitive and prepared to listen. Recognise when things are going wrong. When people don't feel comfortable in an area, they tend to become quiet or aggressive. And the sooner you detect these kinds of adjustments, the sooner you'll be able to preserve that discussion. Sometimes it's possible to reestablish safety, and other times it's necessary to take a break. In any instance, strive to preserve a sense of mutual respect while working toward a common solution. Finally, keep in mind that not having the dialogue is cruel. It's cruel to you, cruel to the team, and cruel to the situation.

Be considerate. It will be difficult at first, but it is preferable to the alternative. And, believe me, it will get easier. Work goes between the cracks when there is a lack of clarity. Work initiatives go by the wayside when there are insufficient resources and time. Great cultures promote getting work done by clarifying responsibilities and encouraging coworkers to help one another. First and foremost, it is your obligation to ensure that everyone understands which lane they are driving in. Each piece of work must be owned by someone. Even if that individual does not actually complete the service, who should I contact if the power washing has to be done? When too many people are assigned to a task, it simply does not get completed. If you are too busy or forget, nobody can help you. Nobody can expect that if you become busy or forget, someone else will just take care of things. At the same time, you want to encourage people to support one another. You mention having a one-team approach. Look, odds are that everyone on your team feels like they always have a full plate of work. If you want to ensure that all of the jobs are completed, you must ensure that your team understands who does what and that employees in your business help one another as needed. So much so that people should attempt to avoid tough talk and make things work.

"Shared rules lead to shared expectations, and shared expectations aid in the development of trust."

A healthy culture is based on clarity and trust, and ground rules help to foster both. So, if you want a healthy culture, set some ground rules for teamwork. This procedure might be short or long, depending on the team. It may just take five or ten minutes for people to discuss how they want to work together and then develop a short list of organisations with a lot of history and pretty healthy fuel. New groups take longer to form because they must go through both a relational list of things like listening and being courteous, as well as a logistical list of things like showing up on time and turning off your mobile phone. At the first meeting of your newly formed management group, the team spent some time discussing how to alternate note-taking, the use of radios and mobile phones, and how to consider the information that would remain in the room against the information that would be sent to team members. After your group has established a set of ground rules for working together, examine how you will keep those ground rules in mind. You would cease activities and return to the covenant, our ground rules, when the tension and irritation reached a boiling point. Do you adhere to these? Are they on your side? Do you want to make any changes? It takes effort to work your way through the ground rules, but it's well worth it. Returning to the ground rules also confirms expectations within your group and explains the sense of unity that groups build when they make a common commitment, even if it is a low-stakes commitment such as retreat ground rules.

Finally, a word from experience. Creating a safe place, respecting all views, presuming positive intent, and questioning ideas rather than individuals are four fundamental ideas that nearly every group I've worked with has come up with in some form or another. If your team completes the ground rule exercise without addressing one of these suggestions, you may want to push them to do so. Fear, particularly fear of failure, will be one of the most difficult difficulties you'll encounter as you attempt to create a strong corporate culture. And one of the most critical processes you can create to foster an outstanding culture is how you evaluate failure.

You may have spent the first half hour providing brief individual updates and the second half hour attempting to address specific urgent issues through a group discussion. Your CFO just informed you that he believes this will be the most productive meeting we hold. You can get a lot done by catching up with each other, asking smart questions, and solving genuine challenges. All of that effort implies that people feel linked to what they're doing as well as to one another, which promotes morale. So, what are your thoughts on meetings? Have you scheduled the appropriate meetings at the appropriate frequency? Have you made the most of your time? Have you made listening to and supporting your team a priority? Being available is challenging and takes time that you may not believe you have, but consider how much time you'll save by getting more out of the few critical encounters. Create room for being accessible in very consistent ways by establishing these basic procedures, one-on-ones, and small team gatherings.

Don't underestimate how pleasant leisure with coworkers may help connection development, trust, and morale when you consider constructing processes to support creating a strong business culture. If you want to build a fantastic business culture, schedule play dates for your employees. You think that by scheduling time for employees to play together, they will form personal ties within the workplace. As people across lines and between levels come to know each other a little better, these linkages assist in breaking down silos. Now, when you explore these options for your own business, please keep one thing in mind.

Leaders may believe that if they do not attend the celebration, it will go better. Who wants to hang out with their boss, let alone their boss's boss? However, this way of thinking is incorrect. Play dates allow you to be a genuine person, not simply a title. So you must attend the party. Remember that play dates aren't merely for making cross-functional contacts. They also foster links between organisational tiers. They are an essential, deliberate chance for managers and directors to meet frontline employees and supervisors. That means you'll have the opportunity to work in the room and get to know your teammates. It is vital to cultivate skip-level trust through building these relationships across levels. So set aside some time and go. Run a quick mental assessment to see whether you already have chances like this in your business. Are they assisting you? Are they creating possibilities for cross-functional and cross-layer relationships? If so, keep going and stay involved. If not, what modifications do you need to make? Remember that your ultimate objective is to create a fantastic business culture, and organising play dates is an important part of that.

At your organisation, you talk a lot about hiring for culture. Yes, every employee has a base level of expertise. But what about cultural fit? It's a major event. You probably spend the majority of your week with coworkers, which is more time than you get to spend with your partner or children. Getting along is a huge thing. You don't have to be best friends, but you do need to build a trusted team that is dedicated to some common aims. While you may discuss mission and culture during the interview, your onboarding process is the first true chance to instil new team members with organisation values. You've been working to improve our procedure for onboarding volunteers and employees at my organisation. After many years of managers trying to onboard their team members in silos, you're moving to a cohort approach that's worked incredibly well for our education programme, bringing on camp workers at the beginning of summer. And for your guest services team, which takes on groups of part-time employees as we scale up for busy seasons.

Most organisations that are rapidly growing employ a similar cohort method, which I strongly recommend. Even more crucial than attempting to onboard people in cohorts, you must create a culture-centric onboarding approach that involves the heart, head, and hands. Allow me to explain.

For starters, people are most interested when they can express themselves emotionally. Engaging the hearts of your new recruits through onboarding appears to be as simple as assisting the cohort in getting to know one another. It entails showing each new recruit how their labour is worthwhile. Perhaps you could share the history of your organisation. Perhaps you could provide some context or explain your motivation. You'll also need to get into their heads.

Onboarding is an excellent moment to outline how work is done in your business. You know that, for better or worse, work is accomplished through collaborative partnerships within your business. And it is critical to help new recruits comprehend this. For you, onboarding is an early chance to establish clear expectations about open communication, collaborative decision-making, and the value of team trust.

Finally, onboarding provides an opportunity to solidify each new hire's common knowledge of your business through active experience. You are not a phantom thinker or feeler. Your new recruits aren't either. You provide new workers with on-the-job training and behind-the-scenes experience. You enjoy meals together and spend the majority of your training time engaging new workers in role-playing. These physical exercises assist in cementing the common feeling of being a part of a team. Get people to play games together or work together to solve a real-world problem. Make anything you do dynamic and purposeful. Remember that onboarding is a vital time to engage your newest, most enthusiastic team members in the type of workplace culture that you want to cultivate. Don't pass up this chance.

You have an open door policy, and people are welcome to interrupt you at any time, but frequent one-on-one meetings have naturally encouraged your team to just drop in for emergencies since they know you're accessible to them to think through all of the other things at your weekly one-on-one. You also have a one-hour bi-weekly meeting for your core operating employees. This meeting, like the one-on-ones, is actually for the team.

You must assist leaders and managers in changing their perceptions of what it means to be productive at work, and this is where meaningful discussions and meaningful connections come into play. Many HR departments at many companies complain that regular interactions (whether formal 1-2-1s or casual catch-ups) aren't happening frequently enough. Upskilling leaders on how to conduct these important dialogues is a common strategy used by L&D teams, but the problem that is typically overlooked is how to enable leaders and managers to recognise the importance of these talks. When workers are given a task, such as checking in with their team on a regular basis, it becomes just that—a task. Building great teams, cultivating a healthy work culture, and achieving desired outcomes all start with trust. The cost of a lack of workplace trust or a culture of trust is much higher than you may realise.

When you arrived on time and prepared for the morning meeting, your entire team was able to work through the problem swiftly; keep doing that. When you arrived late and unprepared for your morning meeting, the whole team was put under a lot of pressure to cover for you. Can you make that right the next time? And then walk away again. Manager Tools emphasises keeping your tone and tempo consistent in each scenario. Refrain from going into too much detail. In our situation, both incidences were minor. Neither of them will require coaching. Both are simple changes that your employee may make. This type of feedback is frequent and timely. It takes the sting out of providing feedback since you've normalised it. When the majority of feedback is good, the authorisation to provide it is more frequently given. It's also important to remember that feedback is about modifying behaviour, not evaluating intentions or assigning blame. You are not providing feedback if you are not attempting to assist your direct report in making improvement.

Please remember to keep the 10X encouraging aim in mind. This was really challenging for me. Do you attempt to avoid confrontation at work, or do you put on your boxing gloves and enter the ring? As it turns out, either reaction will fail miserably. It takes courage to have difficult conversations. When you were a younger manager, your stomach could have knotted up in knots when you knew you needed to have a difficult talk. And all of that worry may be

When seen in this light, analysing all work creates introspective space for improving work relationships and procedures. Finally, remember that analysing without assigning blame does not imply avoiding difficult conversations or lying about how well a project went. No progress will be made until all parties involved understand what went wrong and how to improve in future opportunities. You're working hard to foster a culture in which individuals may succeed, even fail, and continue to learn and grow. Learning to analyse without assigning blame is essential for this process. Avoid the impulse to assign blame. Instead, consider failure to be a wonderful opportunity to learn, change, and progress.

However, as an executive, you have direct reports, and there are teams that rely on my assistance. To provide meaningful help, you must first understand what is going on. Not every detail, but enough background and frame to provide significant assistance.It is your responsibility to serve as an effective sounding board and to assist your direct reports in putting their problems into a broader framework. Look, this takes time, especially in one-on-one and small group sessions. If you want to develop mechanisms that support a great corporate culture, you must be accessible, and by available, I mean frequent holy one-on-ones and small team meetings. If you haven't already started holding these meetings, please do so this week. If you are, I have a few suggestions to make them even more helpful.

To begin with, keep in mind that one-on-one time is not about you. This is an excellent chance to assist your direct report.This might imply that they talked about their weekend for a while. It may appear to be analysing a recent achievement or defeat. It might be dealing with an HR problem. It might be a casual conversation. Regardless, this is a special moment for them as well. How does this appear? Is there anything you can do or refrain from doing to make it simpler for you to work with me? If one of us is out of town, you should try to reschedule the meeting for the following week. If that's not possible, you move the meeting to the next week, but you seldom meet fewer than three times a month. Surprisingly, sticking to frequent one-on-one sessions has considerably reduced the number of drop-in meetings that have occurred.

From Human Resources to Resourceful Humans the need to use human capital has never been greater, with business transformation emerging as the defining phrase for growth executives in the disruption-driven period following the epidemic. Of course, the same development leaders recognize that it is easier said than done if they have not prioritised developing a strong organisation culture that puts people first in the past. Organisational culture reasserts its impregnable position as a vital business lever in this scenario.

The relevance and role of organisational culture have been widely established in a large body of literature. However, there have been several ways to get there. Execution eats planning for breakfast, as they (don't usually) say. To execute a strong organisation plan, your whole team must operate in lockstep, led by shared principles and fervor, and aligned toward a common goal. In short, it necessitates the right kind of culture: one that binds your people together and produces the results you desire. In a PWC study, CHROs, CEOs, board members, and experts from a variety of industries were polled.

Organisational structure, according to 59% of study respondents, is where the significant transition is taking place. Flexibility was seen as a key development priority for employees by 42% of respondents. 52% said they were not confident in their ability to easily redesign organisational structures. Unsurprisingly, 33% of respondents said that employee productivity had decreased. The primary aim for today's leaders is to create a dynamic, dispersed, and inclusive organisational design that is fueled by "whole leadership." Do they have what it takes? Their cultural environment will determine how they build, nurture, and scale.

What is the most effective method for fostering corporate culture?

Culture does not emerge from thin air. It is everyone's responsibility to plant, water, and inspire it on a daily basis. Culture is a dynamic, living phenomenon. It is based on the active decisions we make every day at work. It differs from other corporate assets in that it appears to a organisation's employees, as opposed to, for instance, its strategy deck, finance portfolio, or policy file, which might all be passive or inactive parts. Even when they aren't at their most energetic or expressive, people are never "passive." Culture is something you can deliberately and actively influence, as it can be recharged and reinforced by purposeful and opportune nudges, incentives, and interventions (rewards and reprimands).

Most people are unaware that culture is continually interacting with and adjusting to its external and internal surroundings, looking for windows and chances to sustain continuity. On the other hand, this renders culture sensitive to powerful pressures and "impressionable." As a result, staying "in its lane" becomes a critical priority for leaders. Controlling culture, on the other hand, is easier said than done. While most CEOs are well-versed in strategy and planning, they run into trouble when it comes to culture. This is reasonable because culture isn't something that can be measured with the five senses or quantified on a spreadsheet. It is a (sometimes) mystifying and (always) elusive beast to catch and tame because of its moorings in unspoken behaviour, habits, and standards.

Successful businesses do not happen by chance. They are a result of culture, or a system of shared ideals. Culture does not guarantee success, but it does raise the likelihood of success. Leaders shape the culture as well. Leaders who know how to motivate people, help them realise their full potential, and guide them through challenging situations are significantly more likely to take their organisation to the next level. There is no better moment to start if you are a first-time founder and have not yet thought extensively about the type of leader you want to be. Learning the art and science of culture-building is one of the most significant tasks you can embark on.

The fact is that everything a founder does, especially in the early stages of a business's growth, shapes the culture of that organisation, for better or worse. As a result, it is significantly preferable to be deliberate about the procedure. The following are some of the most critical factors to consider as you work to create a strong, self-regulating culture that will provide your organisation with a competitive advantage.

The vision, values, work environment, and internal conduct of a corporation make up its culture. It is your organisation's individuality. It is in charge of employee perceptions of the organisation, the way it works, and the message it conveys to its customers.

- Why does it stand out?
- How is your organisation perceived? And what is its reputation?
- Why is it important to have a strong organisation culture?

You may fail, regardless of skill or resources, if you do not have a solid business culture. If you look at successful organisations like Apple, Google, Amazon, or Disney, you'll see that their corporate culture has a common thread. They are aware of the values that their brands represent. What message do they want to convey to their customers? They look after their workers and give them excellent perks and advantages. They appreciate their workers' decisions and collaborate with them in a respectful and trusting manner. In an interview, Steve Jobs, Apple's former CEO, stated that the organisation has a strong collaborative culture and does not have any committees. He discloses that they are structured similarly to a startup. They have allocated employees to their various goods and services on an individual basis. Since its foundation, Apple has followed this organisational culture. This demonstrates that Apple was adamant about its corporate culture and how it wanted to operate. They believe in collaborative working, and the organisation's goal is shared by all of its employees. They believe in their product and are proud of it, which shows in their actions.

As a result of its vision and culture, Apple became the world's most valuable technological business. It's entirely up to you how you structure it. Your organisation's ideals, beliefs, and goals transcend your identity. This is when you understand that no matter how far your organisation grows, you will always be a part of it. Use the correct leadership style and concepts to keep everyone on track and to encourage your employee. If providing exceptional customer service or being devoted to your clients is one of your fundamental principles, make sure you reinforce and convey it to your employees.

Your organisation's grasp of business structure and behavior is a quality that your organisation has. As a result, it's critical to work hard to build a culture that aligns with the organisation's mission and values. With this method, you'll be able to help your organisation stand out from the corporate throng. A bad hire may drastically turn the game around for you. Hire people who fit your culture—people who can share your vision and collaborate to achieve it.

When you first start a business, you see a lot of possibilities. The first step is to set objectives and work toward them. You establish a strategy, employ people, and work diligently to attain your goals.

When it comes to establishing a strong corporate culture, having the appropriate vision is crucial. When doing so, you should also make sure to set reasonable, attainable goals. You cannot have irrational ambitions or make promises to your employee that will never be fulfilled. What does your organisation stand for? What issues does it address or resolve? These kinds of questions may appear to be moralistic, yet they are critical for any organisation. It establishes a brand's reputation as well as what it stands for. Coca-Cola claims to revitalise the mind, body, and soul. Coca-Cola stands for this, and it is committed to promoting happiness. Coca-Cola also encourages an inclusive work environment that values the diversity of people, skills, and ideas.

You can't have a great corporate culture unless your people are content and pleased. Ascertain that your employee are happy with their jobs and that they like working with you. Because a workplace is made up of such a diverse group of individuals, it is preferable to conduct an internal job satisfaction survey. A survey may help you analyse and improve your organisation's culture, as well as increase overall employee happiness. Employees that are pleased and content with their bosses and work environment are more likely to put up their best effort to help the organisation succeed.

More importantly, make them understand that it is their organisation as well, and that its long-term viability and development are largely dependent on them. Is your organisation's culture strong? Or do you wish to strengthen your organisation's culture in accordance with its values? If the answer is yes, then this is how you create a fantastic corporate culture. All you need is resolve to adapt to any unwanted change, as well as tenacity and conviction in your mission.

Strong leadership is the foundation of a strong culture. However, in the early days of a organisation, when a first-time entrepreneur is likely to wear multiple hats, it can be difficult to discern what strong leadership truly means in practise. Most young founders have previous corporate job experience, so they understand what it is like to report to a boss. They frequently believe they understand what it takes to be a leader—that management and leadership are synonymous. They are, nevertheless, diametrically opposed. Management is about effectiveness, which is taking something that already exists and making it more efficient. Leadership is about bringing about change and steering people down a new path. Whereas management is concerned with control, leadership is concerned with influence. Management's goal is to gradually improve.

Whereas management seeks to gradually guide people toward a goal, leadership may be disruptive, even revolutionary. Leadership is about understanding when and how to break the status quo. No one, in my experience, works for anybody else; you all work for yourselves. There have been several books produced on how to become a more effective leader. However, in my experience, there are three crucial parts of leadership that are easy to ignore, particularly for first-time founders:

Storytelling is one of the most critical abilities a CEO can have—and one that is rarely taught in typical business schools. There is no better way to connect with other people than through stories, whether for fund-raising, acquiring customers, recruiting employees, or motivating employees. Every day, as an investor, I listen to proposals. The pitches that grab my imagination, generate empathy, and challenge me to imagine myself in someone else's position are frequently the ones that resonate the most. Make good use of the CEO's bully pulpit. It might take years and a slew of failures for some first-time entrepreneurs to grasp how intently people listen to every word they say.

When you're not used to that degree of attention, it may be unsettling, but it can also be quite empowering. It matters a lot to compliment an employee, especially in front of other employees. With this in mind, praise should be made as public as possible, but constructive comments should always be kept private. The only person you should ever criticise publicly is yourself. In that vein, don't be frightened to be exposed. The capacity of a leader to be vulnerable with his or her team may be extremely important, yet it is a skill that is seldom exercised. Most leaders feel that exhibiting any evidence of weakness is a sure way to get fired. However, there are occasions when displaying vulnerability gives sincerity and a sense of shared humanity. It's tempting to act as if you have the solution to everything. The ability to declare, "I don't know," on the other hand, may play a critical role in establishing a healthy culture—and avoiding costly mistakes. You want your direct reports to be candid with you about their own uncertainties and worries. Everyone understands it's safe to let their guard down when you're prepared to display weakness.That is what builds a cohesive team.

"Culture" may appear to be a hazy notion, yet it has a specific meaning: an organisation's common ideals. For better or worse, the principles embedded in a organisation's culture will serve as a guiding light for how employees manage anything from a new client to a crisis response. An organisation that has a strong, well-established culture transforms into a self-policing organism. No one needs to constantly look over employees' shoulders since a common set of values encourages them to make the right decision. When an organisation reaches a certain mass, it is vital to codify its culture. When a organisation has expanded to around 20 workers, when it has created clearly defined organisational roles and opinion leaders in key areas, it is time to codify the organisation's collective value system. So, what's the deal? because the organisation has reached a critical juncture. There is one group of workers that have been with the founder since the beginning. They have a strong feeling of ownership over what they have jointly created, and they are prepared to go to any length to ensure the organisation's success. These "first-wave" startup employees are typically unconcerned with titles or jobs. They understand that if the organisation succeeds, they will be rewarded with a potentially life-changing windfall.

However, at around 20 people, you are now adding a second wave of employees. These second-wave employees are less likely to anticipate personally reaping the benefits of the organisation's success. The title becomes crucial all of a sudden. The role assumes significance. It is necessary to delineate their dominion. If you are not cautious, the second wave of employees might develop a micro-culture that is significantly different from what the organisation has had up to this point. Before they sign on, make certain that the organisation's culture and principles are enshrined in a written declaration. "This is how we do things here," you should be able to explain to newcomers.

Two of the most essential things you must learn regarding cultural codification are: Collaborate with others. Corporations are not democracies, yet a cultural statement is a communal choice that must be made. If an employee offers your culture statement to a new hire with an eye roll, it's generally because it was a top-down, ego-driven edict from the CEO. Instead, co-author your cultural statement with the organisation's other important stakeholders. Discuss what makes your culture special and significant. Make a precise, structured statement about your culture. You will not just strengthen buy-in as a result of this. In my experience, you will also benefit from what your colleagues have learned from their previous responsibilities about what works—and what doesn't—in defining an organisation's culture.

Make your points clear. It is all too easy for cultural declarations to devolve into a litany of jargon and hazy ideals that have nothing to do with reality. For example, at one of my previous businesses, the organisation's culture statement said that urgency should be a vital aspect of the organisation's culture. But, in fact, what does "urgency" imply? A colleague from that business who joined me in my current venture saw that individuals worked 80 hours or more per week to display "urgency." No one was sure what type of behaviour was expected of them. So, working together, we devised a better way to communicate what we wanted our culture to embody: Do now what you may postpone until tomorrow. "Practice what you preach," as the old saying goes. It is equally crucial for a leader to preach what they practise. The most essential thing entrepreneurs can do at times is to advocate and promote the culture they are creating.

You may have noticed a similar thread running across these examples of excellent leadership and culture: effective communication. Communication is always your first and most crucial responsibility as a leader. To do it properly, you must be familiar with the three primary styles of communication. Each has a distinct purpose and should be used in various situations. They are as follows:

One-to-many mode to raise awareness and spread information, such as "this is what we're doing," these are your important efforts, and so on. However, when done correctly, one-to-many communication increases your accountability to your team. Consider it more like reporting to your board than issuing edicts. By your behavior, you are telling your workers, "I work for you, and I am accountable to you." Many-to-many sort of communication serves as a debate forum, enabling constructive conflict. A well-debated conclusion is frequently a good option. Therefore, you should develop a platform where people may question and discuss. One person will always be authorised to make decisions and be held accountable for them, but they should not do it in a vacuum. The idea is for your employees to not just be aware of a decision, but to also believe in it and feel involved in its success. That can only happen if everyone gets an opportunity to express their concerns, objections, opinions, and recommendations.

One-to-one Communication is exactly what it sounds like engaging an employee on a personal level. The purpose here is to foster trust and commitment. You're demonstrating that you care about this person as a person. You are aware of their objectives and problems, and you aim to be an ally in their pursuit of success.

This is not an exhaustive list. There is a lot more that goes into creating a successful culture, and there are a lot of additional questions you'll need to answer to guarantee your business is expanding in the most efficient way possible. However, thinking thoroughly about the culture you're creating—even simply realising that this is a significant question—is a great place to start. The many situational leadership styles, as well as when and how to use them. If you are the first CEO of a new organisation, your career as a leader is just getting started. You have a far higher chance of achieving your target if you are deliberate in your actions along the road.

Understanding and development a successful organisation must have a culture that is founded on a set of deeply held and broadly accepted ideas that are backed up by strategy and structure. Three things happen when an organisation's culture is strong: employees are aware of how top management expects them to behave in each scenario. They feel that the anticipated answer is the correct one, and they are aware that showing the organisation's values will be rewarded.

The backdrop for everything an organisation does is determined by its culture. There is no one-size-fits-all cultural employees that actually embrace the ideals are rewarded and recognised. Employers play a critical role in sustaining a strong culture, starting with recruiting and selecting applicants who share the organisation's beliefs and thrive in that culture; developing orientation, training, and performance management programs that outline and reinforce the organisation's core values; and ensuring that appropriate policies and procedures support those values.

There are signs that it's time for a cultural shift. Culture, like yourselves, is a living, breathing organism that might suffer from illness from time to time. It's crucial to remember, though, that meltdowns don't generally happen overnight; they're the product of a gradual erosion of the values, goals, and forces that have held the team together along the trip.

A cultural matrix frequently throws out telltale signs and warning signals long before it reaches the point of disintegration. It is up to culture keepers to be nimble and skilled enough to recognise them and act with the appropriate response at the appropriate moment.

It shouldn't be difficult to spot such threats to your culture and act before they reach boiling point, whether it's an ambitious effort at change that isn't quite going as planned, a merger or acquisition that has left employees confused about the "big purpose," or a bad review on Glassdoor. If you're alert, it shouldn't be difficult to spot such threats to your culture and act before they reach boiling point. In the marketplace, your brand identity is becoming more muddled. And, when you do appear in public debate, it's not for the reasons you'd want.You're losing top talent to your competitors.

Organisations may spend a lot of effort and money developing a culture, but they may not see the same results—especially if CEOs, managers, and lower-level workers all have different perspectives on the organisation's culture. Employers must ensure that the organisation's culture is communicated to all workers in a clear and consistent manner. In order to build good strategies that support corporate objectives and goals, it's critical to first assess organisational culture. But how do you quantify something as difficult to define as culture? Following the identification of essential elements of culture, such as values, degree of hierarchy, and people and task orientations, companies can analyze culture by following these steps:

Cultural assessments, as well as other activities like cultural audits and 360-degree feedback, can assist in revealing discrepancies. Then, and only then, will leaders be able to erase the discrepancies. If customer service is a component of the organisation's culture, consider how much time employees spend visiting customers' sites, how much connection they have with customers, what customer service training they get, and other indicators of customer service emphasis. Select start-ups, such as AirBnB and Ola, expand and become dominant forces in a turbulent business climate plagued by hyper-competition, while others stagnate or fade into obscurity. In addition, although some huge corporations, such as Google and IBM, continue to innovate and thrive, others, such as Nokia and Eastman Kodak, stagnate or crumble in difficult times. Clearly, size, age, breakthrough goods, or marketing brilliance alone do not determine the long-term success of new or established businesses.

High values and charismatic CEOs, contrary to common belief, are not necessary. Implementing a long-term and disciplined strategy that encourages customer-centricity, financial prudence, continual innovation, and talent involvement leads to holistic success. Such an approach is necessary for building strong and long-lasting organisations.

The process of creating a long-term, non-linear business is comprised of a succession of decisions, actions, learning, and pivots. While the particular procedures differ depending on the business environment, each organisation must pass through five crucial phases, or maturity levels. Each maturity level provides new organisational activities while consolidating old ones. The effective execution of essential practices and their disciplined incorporation into the organisation's culture are required for an organisation's journey across these stages.

The book, "Good to Great," lays forth a framework for transforming a good organisation into a great one. It contains a really helpful model that ties the theories together in a way that is both memorable and relevant. To develop a decent organisation into a great one, you must do everything it takes.

Setting a new direction, vision, and strategy for the organisation, and then getting employees on board, is often the first step in transforming a organisation from excellent to great. One of the most crucial aspects, though, is to get the right people on board and to get the wrong people off. To put it another way, get the proper folks on the bus while getting the wrong people off. Then you'll be able to go somewhere fantastic.

The proper individuals are readily motivated and require minimal management, resulting in excellent outcomes. Hire people that have a lot of character. To make a organisation great, you need a culture that will work for the employees. It seems less like work when you recruit the right individuals who like working together. You won't need to inspire the proper individuals since they will be self-motivated. It is impossible to achieve a great vision without excellent people. If you have any doubts about employing someone, don't hire them.

How will you create attributes that enable your organisation to outperform?

There's no doubt that competition has been fiercer in recent decades. Clients frequently cite it as a critical requirement. Rather than seeing rising competition as a danger, organisations and leaders that want to build a sustainable future through "competitive advantage" see it as an opportunity. While leaders have less control over external influences, leadership effectiveness and organisational culture may be affected and improved in the face of increased competition.

There are a handful, but many of the world's top corporations have failed, downsised, become outdated, or been purchased by stronger competitors since 1985. In 1985, GM and Ford were the world's two largest automakers, but they spent the next ten years hemorrhaging cash, losing market share, and attempting to turn things around. Wal-Mart, Verizon, banks, and technology corporations ousted venerable industrial organisations like ITT, which reorganised and fell out of the Fortune 500. Digital Equipment and Wang Laboratories, two once-dominant computer companies, have virtually vanished. Even resurgent behemoths like Apple and IBM peered into the abyss of insignificance and made painful reforms before fighting their way back to the top.

"As you progress towards enlightenment you will find that you become a winner at anything, not because you are so concerned about winning anymore. You are just concerned about the pursuit of excellence." - Frederick Lenz

Successful businesses frequently fall into three traps that cause their glory days to fade. The first is the physical trap, which occurs when large expenditures on outdated systems or equipment obstruct the pursuit of newer, more relevant investments. There's a psychological trap in which business executives become fixated on what made them successful and fail to recognise when something new comes along to take its place. Then there's the strategic trap, which occurs when a corporation is only focused on today's marketplace and fails to predict the future. Some organisations are unlucky enough to fall into all three traps. There is solid evidence that when leaders operate as an aligned collective coalition, it may have a favorable influence on a team's and an organisation's performance results, as we've seen in organisations.

The simplest method to identify your competitive edge is to ask yourself, "What sets you apart from the competition?" And, more importantly, why should buyers select your products or services over the competition? The first stage is to define and articulate your competitive advantage, then compare it to your competitors to evaluate whether there is enough of a difference for customers to select your organisation over others right away. Differentiating your organisation from the competition might be done through marketable features or cheap operating costs, for example. It ultimately boils down to what your customers desire. Companies are growing and failing faster than ever before as a result of today's rapid technological progress.

It's not a Hall of Shame—most of these organisations are still viable rivals that might one day innovate their way back to glory. Rather, these experiences show how lost opportunities and tunnel vision can throw even the most powerful companies off track. Many businesses, large and small, may benefit from these teachings.

Recognise what's essential to them. They provide products and services that are specifically customised to their requirements. To be relevant and profitable, you must find and preserve your competitive advantages by consistently analysing the market and upgrading your products and services. Although many people still refer to it as the Sears Tower, Chicago's tallest structure is now officially known as the Willis Tower, after a British insurance broker who is one of the building's principal tenants. Sears left a long time ago, and with it, the spirit connected with such a historic structure. Sears helped popularise catalogs, marketed many of suburban Americans' household items, and created durable, cheap brands like Craftsman and Kenmore. Later in life, however, Sears was caught off guard as competitors such as Wal-Mart, Target, and Amazon ate into its market share. As it sought to regain its footing, Sears dabbled in insurance, financial services, real estate, Internet service, and a variety of other businesses.

It might be a financial catastrophe, a disruptive rival, or simply a case of expansion hitting a brick wall. It could also be the outcome of rigorous future planning. The leadership imperative of the twenty-first century may be strategic change. Huron's Innosight established a system for evaluating strategic activities with the goal of discovering best practices that reflect leadership excellence across sectors. Apple, which completed one of the most remarkable transitions in business history but is now focused on executing its present strategy rather than aggressively entering new growth sectors, is one of the most striking names missing from the list. Here are the top ten organisations from a list of twenty that underwent major transition in 2019.

Determine and choose a market sector in which clients have distinct requirements. It might be anything, such as a particular service or place. If you specialise in a service or product that your competitors don't provide, make it available to your customers. Promote your product's pricing, distribution, and locational advantages and strengths. It is critical to sustain your competitive edge after you have achieved it. Maintaining a competitive edge will be easier with a continuous improvement program.

The most powerful competitive edge your organisation can have is a plan that no one else can duplicate. Competitors might copy a competitive advantage based only on products and services. When companies instead focus on building circumstances for collaborative leadership and participation among employees and consumers, they gain a competitive advantage. A distinctive organisational culture emerges when mission, vision, values, and strategic direction are authentically shared and when people are aligned and engaged. Others have a hard time replicating their essence, or DNA.

Founded in 1997, Netflix has evolved from a mail-order DVD business to a prominent streaming video content service, as well as a leading supplier of original content. It has received several international honors for its own shows. In terms of revenue, Netflix is the seventh-largest internet organisation in the world. Blockbuster, this video-rental chain made it through the transition from VHS to DVD without a hitch—until the next big change. When Netflix began shipping DVDs through the mail, cable and phone providers began offering video-on-demand, and Redbox began renting videos for $1 a night through vending machines, Blockbuster was caught off guard. Blockbuster's traditional retail shops appear hopelessly antiquated now that video streams through computers and phones. With a fighting chance of catching up, the organisation is liquidating hundreds of locations, paying off debt, and emulating some of its competitors' practices. However, instead of leading its industry, it is now pursuing it. Netflix has had a string of successes. Blockbuster Video went out of business in 2013.

Dell had a different notion back when IBM and Hewlett-Packard still sold most of their goods through stores: cut out the middlemen and sell straight to consumers. When the Internet came along, Dell took off, and competitors were left reeling as they tried to keep up with its soaring sales. However, Dell began to struggle a decade later as mobile devices began to supplant PCs, low-cost Asian machines slashed profits, and large clients began to expect end-to-end service, not just hardware. Dell has responded with mini-laptops, cellphones, and other popular items, but it is currently lagging behind.

No business marketed the camera as effectively as Kodak did for over a century, with advances such as the Brownie camera in 1900, Kodachrome color film, the handheld movie camera, and the easy-load Instamatic camera. However, with the arrival of digital photography and all the printers, software, file sharing, and third-party apps that Kodak had mostly missed out on, Kodak's illustrious reign came to an end. Since the late 1980s, Kodak has tried to diversify into pharmaceuticals, memory chips, healthcare imaging, document management, and a variety of other industries, but the magic has never returned. Its stock price is currently around 96% lower than when it peaked in 1997.

A "Kodak moment" indicated something worth storing and enjoying a generation ago. Today, the word has become a corporate bogeyman, warning executives that when disruptive technologies encroach on their business, they must stand up and respond. Unfortunately, as time passes, the nuances of what occurred to Eastman Kodak are lost, causing management to draw incorrect inferences from the organisation's troubles. "It is not the strongest of the species that survives, nor is it the smartest of the species that survives. It's the one that can adapt to change the most." Charles Darwin said it best. Eastman Kodak, a longtime leader, declared bankruptcy in 2012.

In 2011, Borders, one of the largest book shops in the United States, went out of business. Why did these once-great-brand-name enterprises eventually fail? It's because they haven't been able to adjust to change. Furthermore, they were unable to unlearn and relearn. Let's talk about the significance of transformation in this context.

Microsoft It was essential in bringing the PC to a wider audience, and it continues to dominate most of the software business. But, like Web TV, e-books, cellphones, and the tablet PC, Microsoft has mishandled or passed over numerous wonderful concepts that others have seised on. "How come none of this was commercialised?" Govindarajan inquires. "Execution is the issue." It's dangerous to stick to one business line, especially in a fast-changing market like technology. And indeed, the market is moving away from the PCs on which Microsoft's software is built.

Motorola's first great success was with automobile radios, which led to two-way radios, which led to the world's first mobile phones being built and sold. Motorola controlled that market until 2003, when it released the popular Razr, the world's best-selling mobile phone at the time. However, Motorola neglected to focus on smartphones that could handle e-mail and other data while newcomers such as Research in Motion, Apple, LG, and Samsung quickly gained market dominance. Motorola was defeated so quickly that its mobile phone sector became a chronic loss leader, prompting the corporation to announce plans to spin it off into a new organisation this year, leaving the main Motorola to concentrate on networking equipment and a few other areas.

Sony controlled the market for TVs, cameras, video recorders, and many other consumer electronics not long ago, and the Walkman was as widespread as the iPod is now. However, as Sony grew into a multibillion-dollar conglomerate with film and music divisions, it lost control of several of its key product lines. The shift from hardware to software, which focused on the brains of the gadget rather than the circuitry, threw Sony and some of its competitors off. As a result, faster-moving competitors such as LG, Samsung, Vizio, Apple, and different cell phone manufacturers—which, of course, also have cameras—have caught up to this old-school innovation.

Sun Microsystems is a organisation that makes computers. It's only a matter of time before luck strikes again. This computer organisation started developing high-end servers just as the computer revolution was getting started, and it realised the benefits of networking and universal software that could run on any machine. Sun's Java programming language, which was released in the mid-1990s and became an industry standard just as the Internet arrived, helped the organisation become a market leader by the late 1990s. However, the dot-com bubble burst, wiping off many of its clients and altering how businesses satisfy their technological demands. Sun spent the previous decade reducing and retrenching as PCs got more powerful and fewer major clients needed Sun's expensive servers. Oracle purchased Sun earlier this year, when the organisation's market value was a fraction of what it had previously been.

In the 1980s and 1990s, this retailer succeeded because its notion of specialty megastores coincided with a spike in American consumerism. As it expanded nationwide, Toys "R" Us pushed out numerous competitors while absorbing others. Then the tables turned, with discounters like Wal-Mart and Target, internet sites like Amazon, and smaller shops with greater quality and service dethroning the once-mighty toy behemoth. Since 2004, when private investors purchased the organisation, Toys "R" Us has been on the mend. Store closures, layoffs, and downsising have all been part of the rehabilitation, with the owners expecting that a public offering this year or next would help collect funds to pay off debt incurred when the organisation was aggressively expanding.

Yahoo! When Web search and aggregation were still new, Yahoo sought to charge for services like e-mail and file sharing, whereas upstart Google gave everything out for free. Customers rushed to Google, which soared to a dominating lead in search that it maintains today. Yahoo evolved into a massive Web site with strong sports, financial, and news coverage that earns billions in ad income, but it also dabbled with job-hunting services, video streaming, original entertainment, and other enterprises that it eventually sold or folded.

Nonetheless, it's still on the lookout for a successful approach, and it's now partnered with Kmart in a sort of faded-glory holding organisation. Analysts believe that when stores close, a Web approach might salvage the organisation. Yahoo's rejection of a $45 billion purchase bid from Microsoft in 2008 now appears to be a massive blunder, since the organisation's market value has plummeted to around $19 billion. Carol Bartz took over as CEO in 2009 with a mission to sharpen the organisation's focus and increase profitability. One of her first acts was to form a cooperative with an old suitor, Microsoft, in order to boost income without the stress of an acquisition.

"Greatness is not in where we stand, but in what direction we are moving. We must sail sometimes with the wind and sometimes against it—but sail we must, and not drift, nor lie at anchor." —Oliver Wendell Holmes

P&G was aware of toothpaste thirty years ago. Gleem whitened your teeth, while Crest protected you from cavities. P & G had more than two brands in several areas, so having two brands in one category worked. They introduced a new brand if they intended to cover a variety of customer benefits.

However, marketing expenditures skyrocketed, making it easier for major retailers like Walmart—who were now in charge—to promote mega-brands. As a result, Gleem was dubbed "Crest Whitening." Mega-brands reigned supreme throughout the 1990s and early 2000s. Niche companies lacked the scalability to make it onto the shelves of large supermarkets. That didn't imply that shoppers didn't desire niche brands; it just meant they couldn't find them. But only for a short time. Both P & G and Nestle had a scattering of mavericks in the 1980s. People would swarm around them, eager to take advantage of their vigor. Others, though, sought to force them out because they refused to conform. Mavericks must be safeguarded. This is something that wise leaders are aware of. They are not treated well by today's evaluation systems, which rely on success on adhering to a set of standardised norms. Mavericks all across the world started to go the way of the woolly mammoth as the millennium arrived.

In the last two decades, neither P&G nor Nestle have produced a breakthrough invention. Their CEOs are bright and inspiring, but a business without mavericks is like a stew without spices. It doesn't matter how wonderful the meat is if it's not seasoned and served with a sauce. Despite the fact that everyone understands that the only constant in the world is change, individuals resist change for a variety of reasons, including fear of failure, criticism, and the unknown. They frequently believe that the devil they know is superior to an unknown angel. They accept the status quo and eventually go extinct. Alternatively, they may fail to adapt to new times and technology, resulting in the same destiny.

Today's Business- companies that are able to find a balance between the expectations of the organisation and the requirements of their employees emerge as winning employer brands. The way we work has to be one of the most significant parts of human life that has irreversibly changed since the COVID-19 pandemic. While companies and employees initially struggled with the work-from-home challenge, they eventually came to terms with it without sacrificing productivity. Now that the pandemic has subsided, companies and employees are realising that the future of work will most likely be a hybrid, a judicious mix of working from the office and working from anywhere, whenever needed. This must be a balance that benefits both sides—organisations must ensure they are receiving the most productive output from their employee, and individuals must know that their employers can provide them with the freedom to work from anywhere whenever they need it. A preferred employer brand, on the other hand, is much more than simply providing its employees with workplace flexibility.

The cloud holds the key to success. Amazon created "Amazon Web Services" (Cloud) to help businesses avoid the high cost of infrastructure. AWS has become a valuable business generator. Amazon has also created a whole ecosystem of products and services that are made possible by its Prime membership, and it is the world's most profitable internet organisation. Keeping a winning streak alive Tencent, a Chinese global conglomerate holding corporation created in 1998, has evolved from an online messenger and video game organisation to a technology organisation with interests in entertainment, autonomous vehicles, cloud computing, and financial technology.

Microsoft is changing the way businesses are run. Microsoft, founded by Bill Gates and Paul Allen, has evolved from a organisation that primarily sold goods, licensing (IP), and devices to a cloud-based platform-as-a-service organisation. Orsted: I'm relying on the wind. This Danish power organisation grew from a state-owned oil and gas exploration and production corporation to become the world's largest offshore wind farm organisation when it went public in 2016. Supporting SMEs with Intuit Intuit has evolved from a product and service supplier to an online financial services ecosystem for small and medium-sised businesses (SMEs). TurboTax is a consumer tax preparation application. QuickBooks, a small organisation accounting package, ProConnect Tax Online, ProSeries, and Lacerte, and several payroll programs are all produced by Intuit.

Moving beyond insurance for Ping An Ping An, a Chinese holding conglomerate, was founded as a financial services and insurance organisation. Its divisions mostly deal with insurance, banking, and financial services. The organisation evolved into a cloud tech organisation that specializes in finance and AI-based medical imaging and diagnostics. DBS Bank is a Singapore-based international banking and financial services organisation. The Development Bank of Singapore Limited was the organisation's previous name until 2003, when it was changed to its current name. The bank evolved from a typical regional bank to a worldwide digital platform corporation based on a "27,000-person startup" cultural concept. It was named "Best Bank in the World" in 2018.

For the past 25 years, Fortune and it's partner, Great Place to Work, have published the Best Companies list, with the last two being particularly tumultuous. While COVID-19 has irrevocably altered the way they work, the greatest companies are stepping up to help their employees navigate unfamiliar seas. Continue reading to learn what makes a organisation stand apart. (Hint: a little more variety, flexibility, and paid time off go a long way.)

long periods of inactivity. employees who felt alone and overworked. COVID was there with everything. Nonetheless, these businesses not only made it through, but also became role models. The message appears to be clear: companies that treat their employees properly during difficult times will attract talent.

Even as the fight for talent heats up, businesses that treat their employees properly in the hardest of circumstances will attract talent. Big Tech now controls Fortune's annual survey of organisation reputation, just as it does our economy. For the third year in a row, Apple, Amazon, and Microsoft are ranked first, second, and third, respectively, for the third year in a row, according to our poll of 3,700 business executives, directors, and analysts. It's Apple's 15th year in a row at the top, a fitting crowning for the world's most valuable corporation. Companies on the front lines of the medical struggle received new respect as a worldwide epidemic dragged into its third year. Pfizer is one of the most effective COVID-19 co-developers. For the first time in 16 years, Pfizer, codeveloper of one of the most successful COVID-19 vaccines, jumped all the way to

No. 4 on our All-Stars list. Danaher (No. 37) made its top 50 debut, with COVID diagnostics and drug-development equipment being critical in the fight against the new coronavirus.

Global equity markets have made a significant comeback since the COVID-19 disaster. As of March 31, 2021, the world's top 100 corporations were valued at a record-breaking $31.7 trillion, up 48% year over year. In comparison, the combined GDP of the United States and China in 2020 was $35.7 trillion. We used PwC data to create today's picture, which shows the world's largest enterprises by market value, as well as the nations and industries from which they come.

Tesla's market value increased by 565%, making Elon Musk the world's richest person for the time being. Meituan, a food delivery platform, and PayPal, a payment processing organisation, both saw their market capitalizations rise by 221% and 151%, respectively, as e-commerce popularity grew. Swiss organisations Nestlé, Novartis, and Roche Holding, on the other hand, were all among the worst ten companies in terms of market capitalisation growth. With a -12% drop, China Mobile was the only business to lose ground. The organisation was delisted from the New York Stock Exchange.

A good organisation is one where people want to come to work every Monday morning, one that clearly defines its purpose, core values, and mission for its employees, and one that fosters an inclusive, enabling environment in which they can achieve their full potential both personally and professionally. Employees consider Amazon to be India's best employer because of the clarity of the organisation's aims, growth prospects, and work flexibility. According to a study done by Business Today, Amazon

India is the best organisation to work for in India. The poll highlighted areas of Amazon's work culture that were strong in the fabric, such as development and learning opportunities, clarity of business goals, and work flexibility.

The India Today Group's Business Today conducts an annual study to determine the top 25 best companies to work for in India. It included topics such as employee growth initiatives, well-being, engagement, and thinking beyond the box. Other organisations in the top ten are Google India, Tata Consultancy Services, Accenture, Microsoft, DHL Express, Adobe India, HDFC, Pfizer Ltd., and Tata Steel. Employees at Amazon India have embraced the Day 1 culture, with each person contributing to making each day a better day for their coemployees and consumers.

What factors contribute to the strength of a organisation's culture?

It's no surprise that many businesses struggle to develop a distinctive and appealing workplace culture. Organisational culture, defined as the shared values, attitudes, and stories that guide individuals inside a organisation, may be difficult to define and develop, not to mention time-consuming. One thing is certain: a positive organisation culture attracts top talent. It has the potential to provide you access to the greatest talent in your business and serve as the glue that keeps your best employees on board. Indeed, 49% of employees would quit their current positions for a lower-paying position at a organisation with a superior culture. So, how can you make your culture one of your most valuable assets?

Adobe, the multimedia and creativity software behemoth, has earned a reputation for valuing quality, innovation, and opportunity in all it does. Indeed's top-rated workplace of 2019 was them, and they've been on Adobe fosters a healthy business culture by providing employees with highly competitive perks such as up to 16 weeks of paid maternity leave, paid time off, and retirement benefits. Adobe also has two organisation-wide breaks each year, one in the summer and one in the winter, during which all employees must relax and recharge. Aside from perks, the organisation strives to foster a culture of diversity, inclusiveness, and justice in the workplace. Adobe thinks that individuals are more imaginative and effective when they feel valued and included. They urge their employees to value each other's differences, to assist one another to be heard, to think about what people can offer to the table, to rethink daily routines, and to stand out for what they require.

Adobe has made a strong commitment to equality and has spent a significant amount of time and effort promoting pay and opportunity equity across the organisation. Adobe does this by ensuring that employees in similar positions and locations are compensated equitably, as well as by looking to determine if promotions and lateral career movements are occurring across demographic groupings. Adobe aspires to foster a culture that values and honors all employees' efforts.Adobe is putting its money on digital experiences. This San Jose-based computer software organisation expanded beyond its core of creative and document tools to include digital experiences, marketing, commerce platforms, and analytics, while switching from packaged software to cloud subscriptions.

Southwest Airlines began operations in 1971 with only three planes and has since expanded to employ over 60,000 people. One of its most prised assets is its culture. Herb Kelleher, the organisation's founder, is credited with establishing the belief that happy employees lead to happy customers, and profit follows. Appreciation, acknowledgement, and celebration are key to Southwest's service culture. Employees at Southwest take the opportunity to acknowledge one another in official and informal ways, such as through internal awards and activities.

"Our values—authentic, inventive, involved, and extraordinary—are founded on the belief that our people and how we treat one another are what make us a great business, Valuing the diverse life experiences that each person brings to work every day is what diversity is all about. It is essential to our success. "**stated Shantanu Narayen, Chairman, President, and CEO of Adobe.**

Considering applicants that will contribute new, fresh, and unusual ideas to your team—"adding" something that wasn't there before—is what hiring for culture add entails. You can establish an organisation of individuals that brings varied abilities, experiences, and views to the table by recruiting for cultural fit, which leads to greater creativity and a stronger, better-performing organisation. Employees who feel involved and informed about critical events and choices are more engaged and driven to perform at their best.

In fact, according to a new Harvard Business Review Analytic Services analysis on workplace well-being, openness and transparency from top executives help to foster confidence among employees. Being transparent and vulnerable also contributes to the development of a trusting culture. And one of the most significant factors in a successful workplace culture that attracts and retains people is trust.

The first area of concentration is a well-defined culture. Your employees should come to work because they want to, not because they have to. The organisation's goal, vision, values, and behaviors must all be identified and branded. What is promoted, discouraged, tolerated, and rejected is shaped by this cultural paradigm. The definition of a culture needs a great deal of thought and consideration. Once defined, it must become ingrained in the organisation's DNA. As we began to act on the behaviors we stated we would not allow, trust grew, and employees began to take personal responsibility for ensuring that behavioral concerns were evident. A study published in the Harvard Business Review in 2018 identified eight different types of culture, and it's a fantastic place to star.

What factors support a healthy organisational culture?

- An organisation's base should be a positive culture. Your culture is influenced by a variety of factors, including meaningful work, gratitude, wellbeing, leadership, and connections.
- Employees should have a strong sense of personal connection to the work they do every day, as they spend close to one-third of their lives at work. They should be inspired to excel in their positions and feel that they have the chance to do so.
- People can grow and feel more connected to their work when they have a vision for their role. Employee engagement and meaningful contribution are improved when they are aware of new and expanded opportunities at work.
- Avoid letting great employee go due to a negative business culture. Celebrate career milestones and accomplishments for your employee as an investment.

Employees who receive personal appreciation from coworkers, colleagues, superiors, and family members feel appreciated.

- A healthy diet and physical fitness are only two aspects of wellbeing. It also includes the social and emotional wellbeing that people experience when they are members of a strong support network. While promoting a healthy lifestyle, your organisation's culture should also promote a healthy sense of community.

- According to our study, loneliness and burnout at work have risen recently. Social media platforms, which were created to connect us, have evolved into interaction platforms.

- Employees are still not as closely tied to their organisation or sharing as many experiences as in the past, though. This disconnect prevents teamwork and might lessen a person's sense of purpose and belonging at work.

- Culture at work is largely influenced by leadership. By fostering employee growth and development via goal-setting, opportunities, and rewards, leaders may reinforce organisation values.

- Encourage employee advancement through frequent one-on-one meetings and ongoing two-way feedback. Employees' faith in their boss grows when they can discuss their job in an open and continuous manner.

Building a corporate culture requires a strong leadership culture. Leadership culture refers to how leaders relate to one another and to the people on their teams. Additionally, it concerns the routine working environment: people's activities, relationships, convictions, and values. Does your intended culture exist as a result of the way leadership affects culture? Are they assisting you in developing a strong corporate culture through the way they hire individuals, construct high-performance teams, carry out organisation strategies, and engage their workers over the long term?

"Without trust, you'll end up with a broken organisation with slow-moving teams. A organisation with a low level of trust is like a jet without gasoline.The cost of a lack of workplace trust or a culture of trust is much higher than you may realise."
-Dr. Amit Das

About The Author

Dr. Amit Das, is a renowned executive advisor, consultant, educationist, author, speaker, counsellor, and coach whose 25+ years of business experience provides high-impact, practical solutions that support his clients' leadership development and organisational transformations. He worked for fortune 500 and left rich leagacy of organising transformational learning workshops. He has transformed more than 5000+ working executives through his path breaking capability building learning workshops. Dr. Amit Das is recognised as an innovative, principled thought leader who combines intellectual rigor and discipline with an ability to translate theory into practice. His operational skills are coupled with a strategic ability to analyse, develop, and implement successful strategies for profitability, growth, and sustainability.

Dr. Amit Das has a successful track record in aligning learning and training solutions to key business strategy with a strong focus on flawless execution excellence to facilitate individual, business divisional, and organisational performance. He keeps relentless focus on measuring training impact and ROI, people capability building graphs, training process governance, performance coaching, and strategic thinking. These have been some of his key individual success traits. His core capabilities include performance coaching, designing training and development frameworks, psychometric assessment and analysis, competency framework development and assessments, content design and facilitation of soft skills and leadership programmes, Learning Management Systems, Learning Impact Measurement, Talent Analysis, and Performance Coaching and Counselling.

Dr. Amit Das has authored multiple management and self-development books, like High Impact Leadership, Redefining Corporate Spectrum, Create Your Leadership Edge, Love-Laugh- Live With Happiness, SMART Parenting @ Zero Cost, Redefining HRM, Building Organisational Capability, Ethical Road Map, Attomic Attention, BYPB, Redefining The Power Of Mentoring, Making The Most Future Fit Organisation, Redefining Talent Management, Defining Your Success Factors, Lead or Plead, Make The Most Of Your Life, Better Half or Bitter Half, Psychology Of Learning And Development, The Transformative Mind & Soul are few of them.

He has a Ph.D. and a Fellowship in strategic learning, along with his first class degrees in Human Resource Management, Marketing Management, International Business, and Corporate Laws from the top business schools in India. He is a certified Psychometric analyst, HR Analyst, OD Interventionist, Human Psychologist, Lifecoach, Leadership Developer, Black Belt (LSS), Strategic Thinker, Talent Analyst, certified professional trainer from the U.K. and certified behavioral coach from the U.S.A.

Dr. Amit Das likes googling, reading books, writing articles & books, cooking, listening to old melodies, and counselling people to unleash their true potential to build a strong nation. He is married and blessed with a son. He would love to hear about your experience after reading his books. You can email him and share your thoughts, or you can use his services for life coaching, positive behavioural counseling, educational support, and mentoring for young, promising students pursuing their B.B.A. and M.B.A. degrees.

References

- *Multipliers, How the Best Leaders Make Everyone Smarter by Liz Wiseman, Greg McKeown, published 2014.*
- *The Leadership Gap, What Gets Between You and Your Greatness by Lolly Daskal, published 2017.*
- *The Power of Positive Leadership, How and Why Positive Leaders Transform Teams and Organizations and Change the World by Jon Gordon, published 2017.*
- *Wooden on Leadership, How to Create a Winning Organization by John Wooden, Steve Jamison, published 2005.*
- *Learning Leadership, The Five Fundamentals of Becoming an Exemplary Leader by James M. Kouzes, Barry Z. Posner, published 2016.*
- *5 Levels of Leadership, Proven Steps to Maximize Your Potential by John C. Maxwell, published 2013.*
- *Real Leadership, 9 Simple Practices for Leading and Living with Purpose by John Addison, John David Mann, published in 2016.*
- *TouchPoints, Creating Powerful Leadership Connections in the Smallest of Moments by Douglas Conant, Mette Norgaard, published 2011.*
- *Organizational Culture and Leadership by Edgar H. Schein, published 2010.*
- *The Practice of Adaptive Leadership, Tools and Tactics for Changing Your Organization and the World by Ronald A. Heifetz, Marty Linsky, Alexander Grashow, published 2009.*
- *Reinventing the Organization: How Companies Can Deliver Radically Greater Value in Fast-Changing Markets*

by Arthur Yeung & Dave Ulrich, Sept 2019.

- *Organizational Theory, Design and Change | Seventh Edition | By Pearson Paperback – 26 December 2017 by R Jones Gareth (Author), Matthew Mary (Author).*
- *The Best Place to Work: The Art and Science of Creating An Extraordinary Workplace by Ron Friedman*
- *Humanocracy: Creating Organizations as Amazing as the People Inside Them by Gary Hamel and Michele Zanini*
- *Fusion: How Integrating Brand and Culture Powers the World's Greatest Companies by Denise Lee Yohn*
- *The Culture Quotient: Ten Dimensions of a High-Performance Culture by Greg Besner*
- *The Insider's Guide to Culture Change: Creating a Workplace That Delivers, Grows, and Adapts by Siobhan McHale*
- *Radical Candor by Kim Malone Scott*
- *Becoming the Best: Build a World-Class Organization Through Values-Based Leadership by Harry M. Kraemer, 2015*
- *Managing Transitions: Making The Most Of Change By William Bridges and Susan Bridges*
- *Our Iceberg Is Melting: Changing and Succeeding Under Any Conditions by John Kotter and Holger Rathgeber*
- *Change Management: Why Weas Leaders Must Change for the Change to Last by Al Comeaux*
- *Doing Agile Right: Transformation Without Chaos by Darrell Rigby, Sarah Elk and Steve Berez*
- *You'r It: Crisis, Change, and How to Lead When It Matters Most by Leonard J. Marcus, Eric J. McNulty, et al.*
- *WorkRules! (Insights from Inside Google That Will Transform How You Live and Lead) by Laszlo Bock*
- *Delivering Happiness: APath to Profits, Passion, and Purpose by Tony Hsieh*

REFERENCES

- *The Culture Code: The Secrets of Highly Successful Groups by Daniel Coyl*
- *Powerful: Building A Culture of Freedom and Responsibility by Patty McCord*
- *The Culture Blueprint: A Guide to Building the High-Performance Workplace by Robert Richman*
- *Leadership: Discover the Qualities of Leaders and How to Use Them in Your Own Life for Ultimate Success by Benjamin Smith, Dec 2016*
- *Lincoln On Leadership For Today: Abraham Lincoln's Approach to Twenty-First-Century Issues by Donald T. Phillips, Feb 2018*
- *The Leader's Companion: Insights on Leadership Through the Ages by J. Thomas Wren, Aug 1995*
- *The Edge of Leadership: A Leader's Handbook for Success by Brigette Tasha Hyacinth, Mar 2017*
- *The Leadership Crisis and the Free Market Cure: Why the Future of Business Depends on the Return to Life, Liberty, and the Pursuit of Happiness by John A. Allison, Dec 2014*
- *Leadership by Values: The Proverbial Cwtch of the Panglossian by Ramesh Subramanian, Aug 2020*
- *Leadership: Essential Selections on Power, Authority, and Influence by Barbara Kellerman, Sep 2010*
- *Leadership 2050: Critical Challenges, Key Contexts and Emerging Trends (Building Leadership Bridges) Paperback – July 24, 2015 by Matthew Sowcik (Author).*
- *2030: How Today's Biggest Trends Will Collide and Reshape the Future of Everything Hardcover – 25 August 2020 by Mauro F. Guillen (Author).*
- *Future Fit: How to Stay Relevant and Competitive in the Future of Work Paperback – Import, 25 May 2021 by Andrea Clarke (Author).*
- *Made in Future: A Story of Marketing, Media, and Content*

for our Times Hardcover – Import, 16 May 2022 by Prashant Kumar (Author).

- *The Future Is Faster Than You Think Paperback – 17 February 2020 by Peter H. Diamandis and Steven Kotler (Author).*
- *Leadership: Theory and practice. Los Angeles, CA: SAGE Publications, Inc by Northouse, P. published 2019.*
- *All Systems Go: The Change Imperative for Whole System Reform (Paperback)by Michael Fullan, published 2010.*
- *The Constructivist Leader (Paperback) by Deborah Walker,published 1995.*
- *Credibility: How Leaders Gain and Lose It, Why People Demand It (Paperback) by James M. Kouzes, published 1993.*
- *Appreciative Leadership: Focus on What Works to Drive Winning Performance and Build a Thriving Organization (Hardcover) by Diana Whitney, published 2010.*
- *Thinking, Fast and Slow (Hardcover) by Daniel Kahneman, published 2011.*
- *The Checklist Manifesto: How to Get Things Right (Hardcover) by Atul Gawande, published 2009.*
- *The Heart of Change: Real-Life Stories of How People Change Their Organizations (Hardcover) by John P. Kotter (Goodreads Author), published 2002.*
- *Harvard Business Review on Leading Through Change (Paperback) by Harvard Business School Press (Compilation), published 2006.*
- *Boards That Lead: When to Take Charge, When to Partner, and When to Stay Out of the Way (Hardcover) by Ram Charan, published 2013.*
- *Innovation in the Schoolhouse: Entrepreneurial Leadership in Education (ebook)by Jack Leonard, published 2013.*
- *Chaos, Complexity and Leadership 2012 (Hardcover) by*

Santo Banerjee (Editor), published 2013.
- *Checklist for Change: Making American Higher Education a Sustainable Enterprise (Hardcover)by Robert Zemsky, published 2013.*
- *Nudge: Improving Decisions About Health, Wealth, and Happiness (Paperback) by Richard H. Thaler, published 2008.*
- *Leverage Leadership: A Practical Guide to Building Exceptional Schools (Paperback) by Doug Lemov, published 2012.*
- *Rethinking Leadership: A Collection of Articles (Paperback) by Thomas J. Sergiovanni (Editor), published 1999.*
- *Leadership on the Line, With a New Preface: Staying Alive Through the Dangers of Change (Kindle Edition) by Ronald A. Heifetz.*
- *We Want to Do More Than Survive: Abolitionist Teaching and the Pursuit of Educational Freedom (Hardcover) by Bettina L. Love, published 2019.*
- *Solving Tough Problems: An Open Way of Talking, Listening, and Creating New Realities (Hardcover) by Adam Kahane (Goodreads Author), published 2004.*
- *Change the World: How Ordinary People Can Accomplish Extraordinary Things (Hardcover) by Robert E. Quinn (Goodreads Author), published 2000.*
- *Practical Approaches to Marketing Analytics in the Digital Age (ebook) by Cesar A. Brea, published 2012.*
- *The Innovative University: Changing the DNA of Higher Education from the Inside Out (Hardcover)by Clayton M. Christensen, published 2011.*
- *Reinventing Higher Education: The Promise of Innovation (Hardcover) by Ben Wildavsky (Editor), published 2011.*
- *Bass & Stogdill's Handbook of Leadership: Theory,*

Research & Managerial Applications (Hardcover) by Bernard M. Bass, published 1990.

- *The practice of Adaptive Leadership: Tools and Tactics for Changing Your Organization and the world (Hardcover) by Ronald A. Heifetz, published 2009.*
- *The Third Side: Why We Fight and How We Can Stop (Paperback) by William Ury, published 2000.*
- *Accelerate: Building Strategic Agility for a Faster-Moving World (Hardcover) by John P. Kotter (Goodreads Author), published 2012.*
- *How Colleges Change: Understanding, Leading, and Enacting Change (ebook) by Adrianna Kezar, published 2013.*
- *Adaptation Studies and Learning: New Frontiers (Paperback) by Laurence Raw, published 2013*
- *More Than 50 Ways to Build Team Consensus (Paperback) by R. Bruce Williams, published 1993.*
- *Adaptability: Responding Effectively to Change (Paperback) by Allan Calarco, published 2006*
- *Building Resiliency: How to Thrive in Times of Change (Paperback) by Mary Lynn Pulley, published 2001.*
- *Playing to Win: How Strategy Really Works (Hardcover) by A.G. Lafley, published 2013*
- *Leadership Without Easy Answers (Hardcover) by Ronald A. Heifetz, published 1994.*
- *Influencer: The Power to Change Anything (Hardcover) by Kerry Patterson, published 2007*
- *Leadership on the Line: Staying Alive Through the Dangers of Leading (Hardcover)by Ronald A. Heifetz , published 2002.*
- *Leading for Powerful Learning: A Guide for Instructional Leaders (Paperback) by Angela Breidenstein, published 2012.*

REFERENCES

- *Theory U: Leading from the Future as it Emerges (Hardcover) by C. Otto Scharmer (Goodreads Author), published 2007.*
- *Complex Adaptive Leadership: Embracing Paradox and Uncertainty (Hardcover) by Nick Obolensky, published 2000.*
- *Invaluable Master the 10 Skills You Need to Skyrocket Your Career by Maya Grossman, published 2020.*
- *Invaluable, Master the 10 Skills You Need to Skyrocket Your Career by Maya Grossman, published 2020.*
- *The Effective Executive , The Definitive Guide to Getting the Right Things Done by Peter F. Drucker, Zachary First, Jim Collins, publish 2017.*
- *The Leadership Challenge, How to Make Extraordinary Things Happen in Organizations by James M. Kouzes, Barry Z. Posner, published 2017.*
- *Backstage Leadership: The Invisible Work of Highly Effective Leaders 1st ed. 2020 Edition by Charles Galunic (Author).*
- *Athena Rising: How and Why Men Should Mentor Women Hardcover – September 20, 2016 by W. Brad Johnson (Author), David Smith (Author).*
- *The Everything Coaching and Mentoring Book: How to increase productivity, foster talent, and encourage success Paperback – January 1, 2008 by Nicholas Nigro (Author).*
- *Coaching and Mentoring in the Asia Pacific (Routledge EMCC Masters in Coaching and Mentoring) 1st Edition by Anna Blackman (Editor), Derrick Kon (Editor), David Clutterbuck (Editor).*
- *Coaching and Mentoring: Theory and Practice Third Edition by Robert Garvey (Author), Paul Stokes (Author), David Megginson (Author).*